St Saviour's Church, Forest Gate

Celebrating 140 Years

Grosvenor House
Publishing Limited

St Saviour's Church
Macdonald Road
Forest Gate
London E7 OHE
Website: https://www.stsaviourse7.org.uk/

This book is published by
Grosvenor House Publishing Ltd
Link House
140 The Broadway, Tolworth, Surrey, KT6 7HT.
www.grosvenorhousepublishing.co.uk

A CIP record for this book
is available from the British Library

ISBN 978-1-80381-346-2

Text: Deborah Fisher with contributions from many Church members
who are referred to throughout the text

Research: Deborah Fisher and Jean Murphy

Dedication

To all those who have worshipped in and served in St Saviour's Church, Forest Gate, and to the memory of Reverend Canon John Williams, vicar of St Saviour's for 47 years.

Acknowledgements

With thanks to: Rev. Cornelius Henry for his enthusiasm and support for researching the history of the Church and for his help in gathering together illustrations; all the Church members who have voiced or written down their memories; Jean Murphy and Ray Vincent for reading and critiquing text; local historian, Dr Mark Gorman, for information and advice; staff of the Archives and Local Studies Library, London Borough of Newham; the British Architectural Library, RIBA; Essex Record Office.

Illustration Acknowledgements

Photographs of:

The demolition of the old St Saviours copyright the London Borough of Newham Heritage Service

The church hall in 1972 copyright the London Picture Archive, London Metropolitan Archives

Parish weekend at Wetheringsett Manor courtesy of Jean Murphy

Church group on Jerusalem trip courtesy of Ray and Pat Vincent

Children's party courtesy of Ambrose Gordon

Church outing 1970's courtesy of Ambrose Gordon

Rev John Williams with his daughter, and in St Saviour's courtesy of Rachel Miller

Contents

Preface

The Christian faith is a historical faith. It is based on the facts of history. Jesus Christ was an actual man who lived and died and rose again from the dead. These are not just beliefs, they are facts of history. For this reason, facts and truth are essential to the faith. Faith is not suspension of the facts. It is trusting that this particular fact of history can change our lives and our world. The world needs the church. The world needs the truth that the church proclaims; Christ on which it is built. Christ is the foundation of the church. He is the cornerstone on which the edifice of the church is built. Christ is who we proclaim and Christ is our sure foundation on which we stand.

In 1882 when the ground was broken to build a church on this part of Forest Gate, the Christians then were continuing the long tradition of seeking to proclaim the Good News of Jesus Christ to this community and beyond. St Saviour's Church was founded to bring glory to God through the proclamation of the gospel truth that Jesus Christ is the Saviour of the world.

The name was chosen to highlight the fact that the man Jesus Christ who lived about 2000 years ago is in fact alive and he is the saviour and redeemer and deliverer of the world.

This little history of St Saviour's church is a retelling of that story and how God by his grace has preserved this church for the last 140 years to be a witness to his grace and love in this community. This history is a reminder to us that God works through ordinary people in time and space. God uses the vessels of clay to show forth his glory. For over 140 years God has been using vessels of clay in the people of this parish to carry on the message of Christ the Saviour of the world to a broken and fallen world.

This book is primarily a retelling of that history, but like all good history it doesn't say everything, and of course there is much that is not recorded or archived in the day-to-day life of a church. But in its selection the book seeks to highlight certain key moments and people in the life of this parish church.

One advantage in chronicling the history of the church is to highlight the many and varied people who have made the church what it is today. The church is a group of people who are called out from the world to be distinctive in their love for God in Jesus Christ and for the world through Him. They represent Christ in their witness to the world and in their love and fellowship with each other. These people are motivated by their love for Christ. This makes the church unique from any other organization on earth. It is a group of people from various backgrounds, class, race, ethnicity and language who have one thing in common, the love of the Lord Jesus Christ. This love and adoration for Christ brings them together to share a common meal as a symbol of their unity in Christ and for one another, and motivates them to tell others about his transforming love.

The history of our local church shows how the congregation has changed over the years – the class, the ethnicity and the language of the people. All these show the changes in the community and it is reflected in the church.

In March 2020, the church doors were closed as a result of the Covid-19 pandemic for the first time since probably the Second World War. For two years the church went through various moments of uncertainty when the doors were closed and our gathering was limited to a few. Most of our worship went online and Facebook, YouTube and Zoom became the media through which the church was kept alive.

The church has again, by the grace of God, weathered another pandemic and we have come out stronger and more resilient. At this moment of writing there is a war raging in Ukraine, there are upheavals throughout the world, changes in the climate that threatens the very existence of humanity, acts of terrorism and the persecution of our brothers and sisters in various parts of the world, economic recessions and depression. The grace of God is steadfast in keeping his church through all the various seasons of life. The seasons will come and go, the upheavals in the world will rise and fall, but God's church has remained steadfast.

Jesus said: *I will build my church and the gates of hell cannot prevail against it* (Matthew 16:18). When the church is built by Christ then nothing can assail it. All the torrents of hell cannot destroy the church of the Living God.

The future of the church of God here in Forest Gate is unknown to us, but whatever that future may be, God is in it and God is directing and controlling the destiny of his church, here in Forest Gate and in the world. The church building may have changed over the last 140 years but the church has remained steadfast. We must distinguish the church building from the church proper. The church is the people, the building is the place where the people gather. The church building is made holy and set apart because of the holy people who gather there. The space is consecrated by the presence of the people of God.

The psalmist says that *unless the Lord builds the house the workers labour in vain, unless the Lord watches over the city the guards stand watch in vain* (Psalm 127:1). This scripture reminds us that God must be central to all of our projects and plans. Without God being central then the plans will fail. It is clear that from the start those whom God commissioned to build St Saviour's Church, Forest Gate, dedicated this to the Lord and this church family was in fact built by God and watched over by God in the ensuing years. And I believe that God will continue to sustain his church in this community for many, many more years to come. May we be faithful to this charge to continue to proclaim the salvation of our Lord and Saviour Jesus Christ to all in the community around us.

Soli Deo Gloria

Reverend Cornelius A. Henry

Introduction

All Saints' Day, 1st November 2022, marks 140 years since the foundation stone of the original St Saviour's was laid in 1882. It offers an opportune moment for a celebration of the Church, and also for capturing more of its history following on from an earlier publication of 1934.

In September 2017 St Saviour's Church held a 'ruby anniversary' to mark 40 years of the Church in its current building and also to raise money for the Church's heating fund. Along with a celebratory meal, prayers, worship, and even a bit of line dancing, a display brought together some of the history of the old and new St Saviour's, including photos, memories, and items from the few remaining Church magazines. This in turn inspired two Church members to seek out and record more of the Church's history based mainly on the records of various parish meetings from the 1940s through to the early 2000s. The previous publication of 1934 had marked 50 years of St Saviour's Church on its site at the corner of Station and Macdonald Roads, so this booklet is an opportunity to update, looking back over some of the intervening decades. It is not intended to record in any detail the contemporary life of the Church except where activities and events tie in closely with themes. References are made to the Coronavirus pandemic which emerged in 2020 and which has been such an extraordinary and impactful event in all of our lives.

The majority of the parish records are inevitably fairly formal administrative records and, because most are handwritten, there is a limit to the level of detail that can be recorded. Sadly, very few Church magazines have survived, in particular some bound copies for the early part of the 20th century and only a handful for the period being studied. But a very important source, of course, has been the memories of Church members that would otherwise go unrecorded. It can be surprisingly hard to recall details and focus them into words on paper after so many years have passed. So we can only do our best with whatever information we have to convey the historical richness, the challenges and developments of St Saviour's Church over the years; the changes, but also the parallels and continuity over the decades. This is not intended as an exhaustive history and there is potential for further research, but it covers many moments and events in the life of St Saviour's Church.

Forest Gate. St Saviour's Church.

A recently discovered postcard marked with date 13/08/09 showing the original Church in its early years

The 'Old' St Saviour's Church

Although there is some overlap with the history published in 1934, it is worth setting out here the context for, and founding of the original St Saviour's Church because of its impact on the Church's continuing history and direction of spiritual travel.

Forest Gate in the late 19th Century

By the late 19th century Forest Gate was changing considerably from its former rural state. There were farms and market gardens around and on Wanstead Flats. Woodgrange Farm, which had 100 acres of land, was growing rhubarb, parsnips, peas and other crops for the London market up until housing developments started in the 1870s, and some market gardens continued for some time after this (Wanstead Flats Working Group 2017).

Much of the impetus for further housing developments was provided by the arrival of the railway in the 1840's. Opened in 1840, the station was closed in 1843 due to lack of use, before re-opening on 31st May 1846 following pressure from local residents (Wikipedia 2022).

A notable figure in the early building developments was Samuel Gurney. He came from a Norfolk Quaker family and married Elizabeth Sheppard whose father, James, owned Ham House which later became the site for West Ham Park. His sister was Elizabeth Fry the prison reformer. The Gurneys moved to Ham House purchased by Gurney in 1812 following the death of his father-in-law. After a successful career in banking Gurney became involved in buying and selling land in Forest Gate, acquiring extensive areas of land in the early 1850's. He was also increasingly involved in all kinds of philanthropic activities, donating land for good causes. From 1855 building developments started on the Gurney and Dames estates to the west and north of Forest Gate

3

Station. Samuel Gurney died in 1856 but within 10 years, the bankruptcy of some of Gurney's descendants in the banking world due to some risky activities, led to the family selling off property to reduce their financial difficulties. 'It was this crash that spurred the rapid building boom in Forest Gate' (E7 Now and Then 2017).

A considerable number of houses were built in the 1880s and 1890s. The Woodgrange Estate, which is now a conservation area, was built between 1887 and 1892 by developer Archibald Cameron Corbett who is remembered in the drinking fountain and trough which he gave to the community and sited in the area known then as the Broadway. These are still to be seen and the trough now contains a floral display maintained by the local Women's Institute. According to the website E7 Now and Then, 'In the late 1870s Thomas – Archibald's father – bought 110 acres of market garden in Forest Gate from the Gurney estate, and began constructing a housing development named after the principal house on the land – Woodgrange' (E7 Now and Then 2018a). The large scale of the Woodgrange Estate, over a thousand houses were built, was unusual in an area such as Forest Gate (Honeybone 2018).

With Wanstead Flats forming the southern end of Epping Forest, the 1878 Epping Forest Act which protected the forest made land in this area more desirable and valuable, and was a strong selling point for those looking to build homes. It would certainly have been an added attraction for those who wanted a better quality of life than was offered by the increasingly crowded areas nearer the centre of London, a life that offered more space and opportunities for leisure to aspirational working class people as well as those better off (Gorman 2021).

Population Increases

In 1852, Forest Gate, including the hamlet of Upton and part of East Ham parish, was made an ecclesiastical district, with a population of 7127. Not surprisingly with all the developments over the next 50 years or so the population increased significantly. Forest Gate was then part of the suburb of West Ham which expanded rapidly over the second half of the 19th century. An article tracing the life and work of a one time resident of Forest Gate makes this statement about West Ham's growth: 'in 1851 it was only a little over a third of the size of Islington, with a population of 34,395, but by 1891 it had mushroomed to 365,134, exceeding the population of Islington and all but four of England's provincial towns, and larger than the Scottish capital Edinburgh' (Pooley and Turnbull 1997, p151).

Religious Influences

During the Victorian period religion was a dominant force in people's lives and influential in social and political issues. It was a time of great change for many with increasing industrialisation and urbanisation. The local church represented a point of stability as well as being the focal point of a whole range of activities, and the Bible provided a moral guide to life in a changing world. The 19th century saw the emergence of an evangelical movement inspired in particular by the foundation of the Methodist movement by Wesley and Whitfield and the Methodist revival of the later 18th century. It also saw the growth of non-Anglican Protestant denominations.

Emmanuel Church, at the corner of Romford Road and Upton Lane, was built as the first Church of England parish church in Forest Gate, and was consecrated on 22nd May 1852. It was designed by the architect George Gilbert Scott to seat about 500 and later extensions in the 1870s and 1880s increased the seating to over 600. Andrew Wilson describes in detail the founding of Emmanuel Church and the extensive area its parish covered (Wilson 1995).

With the rapid expansion of Forest Gate, it was not surprising that there was soon a need for new churches and parishes. In fact, the account of the service for the laying of St Saviour's foundation stone in 1882 opens with the statement:

Owing to the rapid development of Forest Gate, with an equally rapid increase in population, it has long been felt by earnest churchmen that the church accommodation in the neighbourhood was totally inadequate to meet the requirements of the inhabitants.
(Chelmsford Chronicle 1882, p.5)

Daughter churches of Emmanuel were established, the first being St James consecrated in 1882, then St Saviour's consecrated in 1884, and All Saints in 1886. The second half of the 19th century was one of the busiest periods of church building since the Middle Ages. This is evidenced in Forest Gate. As well as Emmanuel and its daughter churches, other churches were being established. Woodgrange Baptist Church, on Romford Road, was built in 1882 and the original Methodist Church on Woodgrange Road, the same year. St Antony's of Padua Catholic Church was completed in 1891. St Mark's began life in a cattle shed before becoming an established church building in its own right in 1894. Some churches appeared as a result of increasing tensions between 'high church' and 'low church'.

Foundation and Consecration

As we have seen St Saviour's Church originated as a mission of Emmanuel Church. Initially services were held in Forest Gate National School sited at the corner of Woodgrange Road and Forest Street on land donated by Samuel Gurney. The 'National Schools' were linked with the Church of England. They were set up by the National Society for Promoting the Education of the Poor in the Principles of the Established Church in England and Wales, founded in 1811, and often referred to as the National Society (Loudon 2012). This school came to be known as the National Emmanuel School because of its link with Emmanuel Church, but later in 1888 the vicar and wardens of Emmanuel Church passed on the role of trustees of the school to Emmanuel's 'daughter' Church, St Saviour's (Wilson 1995).

In 1880 the newly established St Saviour's and this school were housed in an iron building (later also referred to as the

6

'iron room') erected in Macdonald Road on a site which seems to
have been next to the current St Saviour's Church. The building
had a sliding partition down the centre separating activities.
Apparently the partition 'was frequently moved to make room for
the worshippers' (Woods 1934, p.9). There was an obvious need
for a more substantial building and a Building Committee was set
up under the direction of the first vicar of St Saviour's the Rev.
Henderson Burnside. The treasurer was another notable local
figure, Alfred Fowell Buxton Esq. Other members included 'noted
leaders' of the Church Missionary Society (CMS). The Rev. Dr. A J
Carver, Canon of Rochester and Master of Dulwich College was
instrumental in finding a site in Station Road on which to build
the church, near to the corner of Macdonald Road. And it was the
Rev. Dr A.J. Carver who laid the foundation stone on All Saints'
Day, 1st November 1882.

Laying of the Foundation Stone

A detailed account of the laying of the foundation stone describes
the ceremony and the plans being made for the new Church.
A marquee had been erected over the portion of the building
where the foundation stone was to be laid. In a cavity beneath the
stone a bottle was placed containing that day's copy of *The Times*
and *The Morning Post*, a short history of the area served by the
Church, and half-a-crown and a shilling. Among those present
were the Lord Bishop of St Albans and the Bishop of Colchester.
The article from the *Chelmsford Chronicle* describes the plans for
the church designed by Mr Edwin Clare FRIBA, the building work
to be done by Mr J Morter contractor of Stratford, 'the walls will
be of red brick, the windows, arches and dressings being of Bath
stone. The church is arranged to seat about 1,000 people ... The
nave will be divided from the aisles on either side by an arcade of
seven moulded Bath stone arches lighted by a series of clerestory
windows'. The aim was ultimately to have a spire of about
150 feet high though the cost, estimated at £10,000 including
tower and spire, perhaps prohibited this. Without the spire the
amount seems to have been £7,100, only about half of which had

been raised by this point. Psalm 84 and the hymn '*Christ is our corner stone*' were included in the service (Chelmsford Chronicle 1882).

It is clear in the account of the ceremony that only half of the money required to build the Church has been raised and hope is expressed that those 'who have made their wealth in the neighbourhood and diocese will not allow the work to stand still for want of funds' (Chelmsford Chronicle 1882, p.5). Another article written later on in the decade and headed 'St Saviour's Church Debt' indicates that, perhaps not surprisingly, the shortfall continued for some time. The article describes a concert 'given in the iron room adjoining the church ....The profits were devoted to refunding the debt upon the church expenses account' (Stratford Express 1888a, p.3).

The Church was consecrated on 1ˢᵗ April 1884 by the then Bishop of St Albans, Bishop Claughton, but no first-hand account of this event has so far been identified. The Jubilee booklet gives some account of the clergy present and the reverends who delivered services in the first few weeks (Woods 1934). The iron building in Macdonald Road became increasingly dilapidated, was sold for £25 in 1892 and as it was being demolished, was badly hit by an overnight storm (Woods 1934).

St Saviour's Parish

A separate parish, taken from Emmanuel, was then formed in the same year. The plan attached to the Order-in-Council of 11ᵗʰ August 1884 shows that the new parish covered all or part of the following streets: Bective Road; Bignold Road; Brownlow Road; Chapel Street (*possibly Chapter Street*); Clare Road (*now Clare Gardens*); Cobbold Road (*now Clinton Road*); Dean Street; Derby Street (*became Oakhurst Road in 1897 but disappeared in development of Lord Lister Health Centre and flats in 1960s/70s*); Essex Street; Field Road; Forest Road; Forest Street; Fowler Road; Ingestre Road; Leonard Road; Leyton Road (*became Dames Road in 1887*); Macdonald Road; Norfolk Street; Odessa Road; Station

Road; Stracey Road; Stroud Road (*probably Strode Road*); Suffolk Street; Sydney Road; Talbot Road; Vansittart Road; Wellington Road; and Woodgrange Road otherwise Woodford Road (Essex County Record Office Reference: D/P 631). At this time the church was in the Diocese of St Albans which covered Essex and Hertfordshire. It was in 1914 that the Diocese of Chelmsford, in which the Church now sits, was formed.

Church Hall and Vicarage

The Jubilee booklet paints some picture of how the space in the old St Saviour's was being used to capacity:

> The work in the Church went steadily forward, the Church frequently being full to overflowing, and chairs were placed in the Nave and the Aisles; and the work among children continued to expand. Temperance work, Services of Song, Lending Library for Sunday School children, Debating Societies, Choral Societies, and other efforts all assisted...
>
> (Woods 1934, p, 15).

The need for a separate church hall was increasingly felt especially after the closure of the National School Buildings in 1895. The Jubilee booklet says about this: 'Church Day Schools for Infants, Girls and Boys were held in the Forest Street Buildings, and were well attended up to the opening of the Whitehall Place Board School (where a fee of 2d. per week was made). After this the deficit in the working expenses increased year by year until they were closed for want of funds in April, 1895' (Woods 1834, p.38). The Whitehall Place Board School was the forerunner of what is now Forest Gate Community School (BHO: British History Online 1973). A railway arch at 365 Station Road was already being used as the Boys School and also acted as the parish hall, the noise from regular passing trains being far from ideal. From 1892 there were attempts to acquire land in Macdonald Road next to the Church site and in 1896 the Church trustees acquired some land here for school buildings (Essex County Record Office D/P 631; Woods 1934).

The Reverend Alfred N. Rae who was instituted as vicar of St Saviour's on 10th June 1903 oversaw the building of the church hall designed by F. Danby Smith ARIBA. It is described in *Buildings of England* as 'a striking and original building in the Arts and Crafts manner' (Cherry et al 2005). The Church Magazine of June 1904 conveys the excitement of this moment:

> Scaffolds, poles and planks, bricks and mortar, foundation digging and laying are the sights and sounds which herald the month of June in our parish. Our new schools are being erected ... hopes are raised high and the spirit of cheerfulness is displayed on the faces of Vicar, Wardens, church officers and, not least amongst them, the church workers (i.e. Sunday School teachers). And, we need hardly say it, the Sunday School Scholars.

On the 17th June 1904 the foundation stone of the hall was laid by Alfred F Buxton. Books of 60 perforated slips each representing a brick were sold to raise money. On 21st October 1904 the hall was opened by the Lord Bishop of St Albans. The stones recording both events remain on view today. It is a significant moment in the history of the Church. The drama of the moment is conveyed by the Rev. Rae in the November Church Magazine:

> The Building in which the Sunday Schools of St Saviour's and all the organisations of the parish could be held, and through which the long-looked for abolition of the Mission Room could be brought into effect, and which has been for many years the luring vision, and one might say, had become a bye-word, does at last, to the delight of all, stand in Macdonald Road in full view and complete, and is one of the finest Church Halls in Forest gate, worthy of the church and the parish.

A very simple programme of the opening ceremony is held by the Essex Record Office (Ref D/P 631/6/5). On the front cover is the text 'Form of Service for the Opening of St Saviour's Hall, Friday

Afternoon October 21 1904'. The service consisted of three hymns (hymn numbers only); Psalm 127 and two sets of prayers written in full; an address; and a final blessing. The back cover is blank.

In the 'Vicar's Letter' in the Church monthly magazine for 1st July 1906 the Rev. Rae talks about two schemes set afoot to reduce the £350 remaining debt for the hall. One scheme involved collecting at least ten shillings from church members by September 12th of that year, or donating that amount if not collected. The other scheme 'is Mr Haydon's, that you promise to give a shilling a week, and he will call for it each week.' This was followed by text urging church members to consider their duty and the value of the hall to them and their children, 'remember it is not for ourselves only that this Hall was built, but chiefly for God's work'.

At the same time there was a call for a vicarage to be built near to St Saviour's. It is clear from the Jubilee booklet that attempts to raise money for the hall and vicarage were difficult and were made harder by the impact of the South African War from 1899 to 1902. But money was made from the sale of the Forest Street Schools in 1900 and invested by the Charity Commissioners. The newly married Reverend Rae and his wife had made their home in Sprowston Road initially and there is earlier mention of some accommodation in Windsor Road. A vicarage was eventually built in 1910 in Sidney Road.

Local School uses Hall

In the sixties use was made of the church hall by Forest Gate County High School (now Forest Gate Community School). A Hall Management Committee was set up in 1960 and is still referred to in 1963. At a PCC meeting on 6th November 1961 a proposal that the hall be used between 9am and 4pm for PE exercises for two years while the school is being rebuilt was agreed in principle. In the minutes of 15th January 1962 we learn that the hall is also being used for technical drawing classes.

There seem to have been some concerns about management of the heating system. In February it was stipulated that a person must be prepared to undertake the stoking of the fires required for the system. Though in the following month a comment was made that fires are not being lit and there is still concern in September 1962. Other conditions are that users of the hall would need to be as quiet as possible while meetings are taking place in the small hall. Also that the school would not be able to use the hall a week in advance of the annual bazaar – and we will later see how important this bazaar was in the life of the Church and its community.

In minutes of the 28th October 1963 there is a reference to vandalism – 'wrecking' of the piano in the small hall and damage to chairs – culprits not known, though there is some question as to whether it might have been caused by school pupils as the school is still making use of the small hall at this time. On 25th October 1965 we read that Newham has offered £35 towards repairs to the damage in the hall sustained during the occupancy of the school.

Church Garden

There are a few mentions of the garden of the old St Saviour's and an on-going concern over its upkeep. At the meeting of 20th July 1955 'the question of care, or lack of care, of the church grounds was raised', the garden was becoming an 'eyesore'. In April 1957 there is an appeal for help with garden maintenance. By June it is agreed to try and find a person to maintain the garden for some payment. The minutes of the 30th August 1957 record that an offer of some garden tools has been made to the Church, and a temporary paid gardener has been found. Church members are invited to donate rose bushes in memory of friends. By December, 18 have been donated and a plan has been drawn up for a rose bed. The trees that are currently surrounding the St Saviour's Court flats we see in photographs and drawings of the Church in the sixties and seventies and are likely the ones recorded as being planted in 1893. It is also recorded that the privet hedge that we see in some old photos was planted in 1926 (Woods 1934).

War Damage

During the Second World War two episodes of damage are described. Damage to the roof in 1940-41 caused a considerable amount of sand to fall into the mechanism of the organ. In 1944 the Church was damaged on the night of 19th July when a flying-bomb fell in Clare Road. The roof on the north side of the Church was severely damaged, many windows broken and the roof structure of the north aisle fractured. Although the Church continued to be used during the summer, in October 1944 it was closed and services took place in the hall, 'which, although it did not escape damage was readily convertible into a church, and was duly licensed by the Bishop'(Annual report 1944-45). The knock-on effect of damage to the roof had lasting consequences, for example rain damaged the electrical system, the organ, kneelers and many other items. A new boiler and heating system was needed at the cost of £500. Delays in repairs were expected as 12 churches in the Diocese had been destroyed and 230 damaged.

An appeal was made for a General Restoration Fund setting the target at £2000. The vicar at this time was BC Aldis. A letter of June 1946 states that although the War Damage Commission will meet the cost of repairing the bomb damage, 'it is extremely doubtful if it will pay more than a small portion of the cost of reinstating the Church to its former condition'. An appeal is therefore made to the parishioners and friends of St Saviour's who 'have never failed to rally to the support of their church in the past'. In a slim St Saviour's Church Yearbook for 1949-50 a letter from the vicar confirms that over £1400 was raised in two years. As a result:

A new heating installation and a new electric lighting system have been installed; the organ has been completely overhauled, the windows have been replaced, the Church has been cleaned from top to bottom, and a host of minor repairs attended to. A new fence has been erected around the Church, the gardens are being re-laid out, and now the Church stands ready to be re-opened ...

The 'Re-opening Service' took place on the 2nd July 1949 at 3pm conducted by the Rt. Rev. The Lord Bishop of Chelmsford. It was followed at 4.30pm by a 'Reunion Gathering' in the hall. As part of the event Psalm 118 verses 19-29 were sung along with the Hymns: 'Now thank we all our God', 'Great Shepherd of thy people, hear', 'Christ is our Corner-stone'. There was a dedication of three memorials: the F.W. Woods Memorial Tablet, The A. Moorby Memorial Bible and the T.R. Page Memorial Clock. The annual reports of this time record that the memorial to Frederick William Woods, twice warden and author of the 1934 history of St Saviour's, acknowledged that he 'faithfully served God in this parish from 1881 – 1940'. A letter in the archive written by a relative in July1949 expresses their pride at the memorial and their pleasure at the re-opening of the Church. A.R. Moorby had died in active service and the Bible was a gift of his relatives. A letter of 23rd July records that some photos were taken at this ceremony of the procession which included the Bishop, choir and wardens.

St Saviour's remembered the members of its community who had lost their lives in the two world wars. The archives have a copy of the programme for the 'St Saviour's Church War Memorial Service of Unveiling and Dedication' held on Saturday 19th November 1921 at 4pm. The service included two hymns, Psalm 103, a reading of Wisdom III 1-6, and the 'Last Post' and the 'Reveille' were played. The dedication was made by the Bishop of Barking. The cover of the service programme shows the memorial, and the names of those lost from the community in World War I are listed in the programme. The annual report for 1949-50 records that a tablet to the memory of all the men, women and children of the Church and parish who lost their lives in the 1939-45 war is to be unveiled in May 1950. The 1950-51 report further states that the names of all of these parishioners should be recorded. It was decided that a list of the names would be made, to be kept in a glass-topped case near the memorial.

Sadly the 1914-18 memorial did not survive the demolition of the old St Saviour's and this is confirmed in the minutes of 11th September 1995 when church warden, Ken Jupp, proposed that a permanent record be kept in book form. Ray Vincent has some memory of discussions around the difficulty of saving the memorial and resiting it. There was insistence that at least a photograph of it be taken. The minutes for 4th December 1995 confirm that the records of those lost in the two world war books are now in one case. We presume the glass topped case which is now fixed on the wall at back of the Church containing records for both wars is the one also referred to in the 1950's. This display case also includes the book recording those lost in both wars in the parish of St James's Church. St Saviour's also has the wooden plaque which records those in St James's parish who died in World War II, arranged according to the different armed services with a separate list for civilians.

In May 1946 the iron railings and gates that had been erected round the Church and the hall in 1926 at a cost of £150 were requisitioned by the Ministry of Works under the provisions of the Defence of the Realm Act, for salvage purposes. The Church was able to claim for some compensation for this in February 1949.

Station Road in the 1960s and 1970s

Since the 1880s Forest Gate had been within the County Borough of West Ham. In 1965 the County Boroughs of West Ham and East Ham were abolished and the areas united to form the London Borough of Newham. In an article from the *Newham Recorder* written to mark the retirement of Reverend Canon John Williams in 2012, he remarks on the poverty of the area when he started his ministry in 1965: 'there was a lot of poverty after the Second World War, most people didn't have a bathroom, a phone, or a car' (Kvist 2012). Between 1951 and 1981, Newham's population shrank by nearly 30 per cent owing to factors such as wartime evacuations, as many did not return, and also increasing unemployment.

In the last few decades of the old St Saviour's there was still something of a village feel about Forest Gate, it was almost a self-contained community. A local historian, Carol Johnson, who contributed regularly to the community newspaper, *The Forest Gate Times*, and who lived during her childhood in Macdonald Road, remembers this village feel. And especially in Station Road which provided about 60 shops and businesses and three pubs, with the school at the end of the road, enabling residents to do much of their shopping in Station Road rather than nearby Woodgrange Road (Johnson 2003). A Newham report of 2009 looking back, describes the old St Saviour's parish as 'a vibrant, well-knit community'(London Borough of Newham 2009, p.11).

So the old St Saviour's was in the centre of this busy community and, as a relatively large building with its surround of trees, would have stood out amongst the small terraced houses and shops. Whether it was weddings, christening or funerals, Sunday School or young people's clubs, most local residents would have made use of St Saviour's at some time, even if not regular attenders. Anne and Albert Gordon remember that the Church was full of children with so many families attending. The Christmas carol service is always a popular one and it is likely that many attended that as, even in more recent decades, there have been times when the new St Saviour's was full for this service.

Long-time Church members who married in the old St Saviours are Georgina Leadeham in 1966, and Ray and Pat Vincent in 1967. Ray remembers that the vicar, John Williams, came back from his holiday to marry them and ended up carrying out another marriage service on the same day.

We have some small insights into the demands of what must have been quite a densely populated parish by the sixties. In the PCC meeting of 1st February 1957 a statement was minuted after the Reverend and Mrs Blake left the meeting stating that, 'although in no way wishing to minimize the work done by Mr Blake we as a council feel that the primary need is for a younger married man to undertake this very difficult parish. There is a special need for one who will work among young people and undertake real pastoral visitation'. Echoing this, the next vicar of St Saviour's, the Reverend Hampton, gave a personal announcement recorded at the meeting of 21st July 1964, that he was thinking about retiring but had accepted a living in a small country parish. He stressed that he was not unhappy in the parish but 'felt that a younger man with a lot of vim is needed in the parish'.

An interesting and unexpected insight into a local business is given in records of a PCC meeting on 28th October 1963 when a Mr Warner of Station Road is given permission to hold a wallpaper display in the church hall on three afternoons and evenings during school half-term. Also, in the archives there are letters dated August 1960 from J D McDougall Limited, a textile company at 64 Station Road, asking if they can use the hall occasionally for marking and shaping canvas cloths when they need a floor larger than that available at their premises. Permission is given for occasional use. This company, which has been supplying stage scenery companies internationally for over 100 years, still exists and is now based in McGrath Road E15.

However, as the sixties and seventies came and went, there were definite signs of change in Forest Gate. Some housing was demolished, partly under the guise of slum clearance, to make way for flats and new housing estates. It seems symbolic of this change that the seventies also saw the demolition of the old St Saviour's.

The original St Saviour's

Stone marking the foundation of the church hall 1904

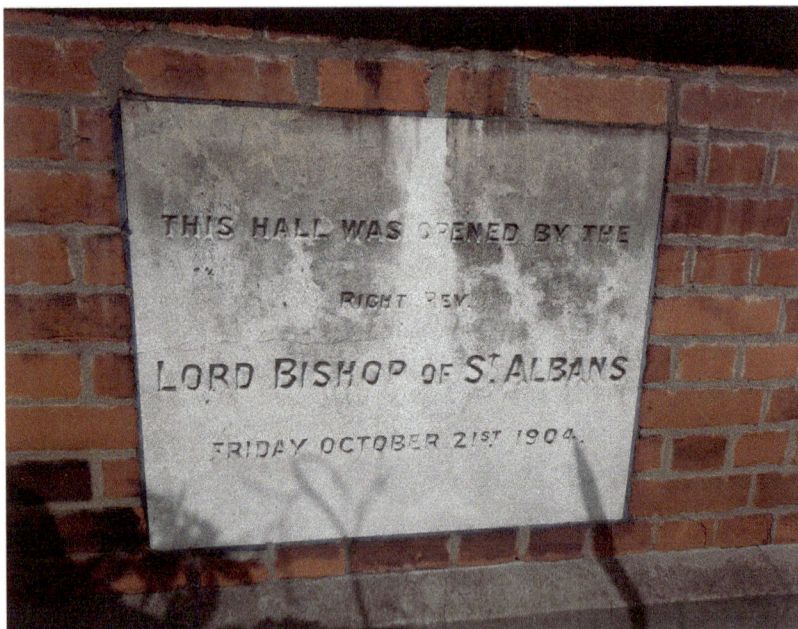

Stone marking the opening ceremony of the church hall 1904

The church hall in 1972 (copyright The London Picture Archive)

St. Saviour's Parish Church
FOREST GATE

REOPENING
JULY ———— 1949

SATURDAY, 2nd JULY

3.0 p.m. **Reopening Service** conducted by the
Rt. Rev. the Lord Bishop of Chelmsford

4.30 p.m. **Reunion Gathering** in the Hall

SUNDAY, 3rd JULY

8.0 a.m. **Family Communion Service**

11.0 a.m. **Parade Service** Preacher: The Vicar

3.0 p.m. **Children's Service**
Preacher: R. Jenkins, Esq.

6.30 p.m. **Evening Service**
Preacher: Rev. R. Williams

THURSDAY, 7th JULY

7.30 p.m. **Confirmation Service**
The Rt. Rev. the Bishop of Barking

The Reopening Service in 1949 following closure due to bomb damage

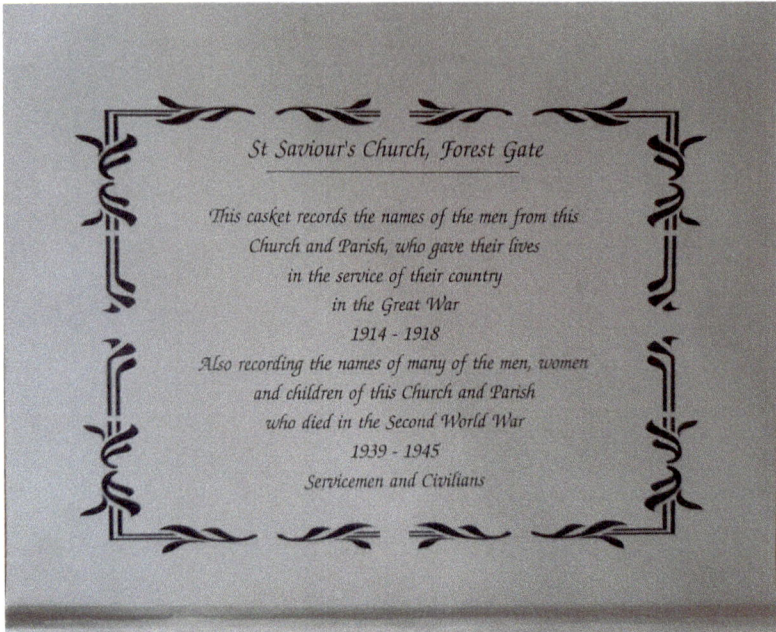

Top sheet of St Saviour's War Remembrance display case

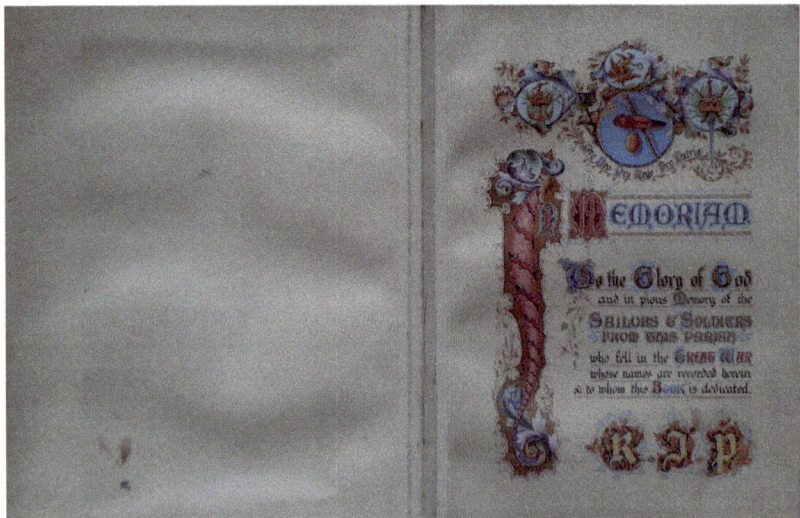

Opening page of St James's War Remembrance Book

Demolition of St Saviour's in July 1975
(copyright London Borough of Newham Heritage Service)

Demolition of St Saviour's in July 1975
(copyright London Borough of Newham Heritage Service)

The 'New' St Saviour's Church

The capacity offered by St Saviour's combined with its church hall which was such a strength in its early years, was to become, as times and population of Forest Gate changed and church-going diminished, a key reason why the building of 1884 did not survive.

Planning for a New Church

The PCC meetings minutes record some of the thought-processes, decision-making and planning leading to the development of the 'new' St Saviour's. The minutes through the 1950s, 1960s and early 1970s convey a picture of mounting and costly structural problems – dry rot, frequent roof repairs, damage from pigeon droppings, reports of the cold and draughtiness so severe that the church hall had to be used instead for services in winter, except for Communion services. Administrative archives over the decades with extensive correspondences, quotes and invoices from a whole range of companies, especially about the heating system and roof repairs, add further to the picture.

An overriding consideration was that the Church was now too big to comfortably serve the congregation. For example, on 23rd October 1953 it was agreed that a curtain be put across the nave to bring the congregation together at the front of Church. Much later on 6th August 1965, for the same reason, it was decided to rope off the back pews. From 1970 most Church services were being held in the church hall (Dunhill 2016). By this time Canon John Williams had become vicar of St Saviour's and remained for well over 40 years, retiring in 2012. The meeting of 6th August was the first one that he chaired.

For a time discussions about repairs were set aside because of a proposed amalgamation of St Saviour's with St James'. By

November 1967 it was clear that this proposed amalgamation would not take place and that repairs to the Church now need to be reconsidered. In fact it is suggested that a long term view be taken to consider the whole question of the church building and that a special committee be set up for this purpose. On 22nd February 1968 members were elected to this special committee to consider the future of the building. Again, with reference to the size of the Church, the committee was asked to look into organising a special small space for Communion when attendance was small. There had been a proposal that choir stalls be used for this. But in the end any idea of partitioning the Church was found to be impractical. The committee was also tasked with looking at heating for both Church and hall.

All of this suggests the seriousness of the overall state of the Church. A current member of the Church, Ray Vincent, who sat on the building committee, sums up his experience then in one sentence: 'the 'old church' was large, cold, damp and depressing and a normal congregation would get lost in the church.' A new church seemed inevitable. At the minutes of the PCC meeting of 4th March 1970 the following statement is made: 'We regret that the present Church building is too large for our present needs, yet feel that we have no alternative but to accept in principle the architects outline plans for the building of a 'new church', sixteen maisonettes and garages on the church site'. Although regret was definitely expressed by some present, there was nevertheless unanimous agreement to the decision. It was then ratified at the AGM of 31st March 1970.

By the PCC meeting of 19th August 1970, a new plan was being discussed as the original plan for three storeys of flats, along with some garages, had been turned down due to light issues. Meanwhile planning was progressing for the new St Saviour's. In November 1970 consideration was given to a proposal that the church hall be divided into two floors, the upper floor to be a hall. But the minutes of 23rd September 1971 detail a new plan to convert the main church hall into a church to provide seating for

200 with suggestions that the entrance lobby be widened, the kitchen modernised and the small hall enlarged. The scheme was to be self-financing, because of the sale of land for the building of flats. It would be necessary to raise money only for the organ and for furnishings of the church hall.

During the 1970s, two priority issues in the PCC and annual general meetings were management of the plans for the new St Saviour's and also for the proposed union of the parish of St Matthew's, West Ham, with that of St Saviour's. In 1972 John Betjeman made a visit to both churches on behalf of the Council for the Care of Churches. St Saviour's was one of two churches designed by the architect Edwin Clare FRIBA, the other being St Bartholomew's Church, Shepperton Road, Islington. Designed in 1863, it was demolished in 1970 which perhaps meant that an even more careful assessment needed to be made of St Saviour's and what should be retained. Ray Vincent remembers that Betjeman loved the church hall. During the summer of 1971 the church hall was being used for worship and a decision was made not to hold any more weddings in the old Church. Interestingly a meeting in August 1973 records a suggestion that 'something might be done to brighten the exterior image of the hall since it was neither conspicuous as such, nor very inviting'. We are aware today that some people walking along Macdonald Road, and even living in the road, do not recognise the St Saviour's building as now being a church because it does not fit the stereotypical image of a church.

The DCC meeting of 22nd May 1975 recorded that the demolition of the old Church was to go ahead and this took place in July 1975. Meanwhile estate agents were negotiating sale of the site. It also recorded that Mr Dunhill was looking at the cost and possibilities for the installation of the organ from the old Church into the new Church (more about this in the section on music in the Church). Various aspects of the re-design were discussed at the meeting of 20th September 1976. There was a decision to put a cross on the outside of the building and subsequently a number of emergency meetings were held to decide its design. It was not until late 1978, as reported in the minutes of 13th November 1978, that the cross was erected and it was intended that it be floodlit. It was decided that the boundary fence would be a three-foot prickly hedge, with gates and fence of the same size 'to discourage vandalism' but still allow the Church to be very visible. The building work on the new Church commenced in February 1977. Bricks from the demolished St Saviour's were used in the building of the flats on the site and possibly for additions in the transformation of the hall to the new St Saviour's. The good features of the former church hall, with the additions and changes now made had been, according to Betty Osborne then lady worker at St Saviour's, 'superbly exploited to make a simple but dignified Parish Church, full of light and warmth and beauty' (Osborne 1978).

Consecration of the 'New' St Saviour's

The DCC (District Church Council) meeting of 13th June 1977 confirmed the date for the consecration of the new Church by the Bishop of Barking on 15th October 1977 with a list of who should be invited – Archdeacon, Deacon of West Ham, Deanery clergy and workers, patrons, clergy from the Forest Gate Council of Christian Churches, mayoress, member of Parliament, Mr and Mrs Barnard, the architects and contractors. The press and local radio were to be informed. The actual service was to commence at 3pm followed by tea, biscuits and cake, and an Order of Service would be printed.

Betty Osborne (1978) describes the drama of the day as a crowd waited outside for the service to start:

> The procession had joined us at the front door, and there was a hush as the Rector invited the Bishop of Barking to consecrate the new Church. The Bishop raised his staff and knocked on the door. Mr. Millard, the architect opened it, and asked the Bishop to offer his design, and the work of the builders to God.

Then the Bishop, the Chancellor and other dignitaries followed by the staff and all the people entered the Church singing, 'O enter thou His gates with praise'.

So the 'new' St Saviour's now took up the space of what had been the main hall, and the small hall continued as the church hall with later additions and a modernised kitchen area. Osborne (1978) describes the building we are familiar with now, 'an outer vestibule having a small room on either side and an inner reception area under the newly constructed organ pipe platform'. She describes the large plain wooden cross above the altar 'visible to all through the glass-panelled doors'. Two small rooms opposite each other were also built into what was now the Church at the altar end, and these became the vestry and a small classroom. A plaque above the inner door of the Church commemorates the day of the consecration.

With the old Church being demolished in 1975 and work being done in the church hall to create the new St Saviour's, there were some chaotic times. At the AGM of 26th April 1977 thanks were given to the congregation of St Saviour's for coping with the building problems. The new building had emerged after 'eight months endurance of services among, dust, rubble and mud, piles of bricks and bags of cement', with lighting provided by bulbs hung from a scaffold (Osborne 1978). The first AGM that followed the consecration of the new St Saviour's was on 11th April 1978 and it was noted that during the chaos, the work of various groups had been able to continue through meetings in private houses and at the rectory. Seven to eight years of planning and work had culminated in an encouraging autumn outreach, prior to the consecration service and 'spiritual growth had been evident as well as the building of brick and mortar'.

Church Garden

St Saviour's, on its current site, is lucky to have a reasonable-sized and attractive garden. Many churches in London do not have the luxury of a garden. It is something to be treasured. In October 1978 there is mention of having a rota for garden maintenance but it was thought to be impractical. An application had been made for soil from Newham parks department.

By the late 1980s the garden had undergone a bit of a renovation as at the AGM in April 1989 the vicar remarks that it had been one of the most encouraging years since he started at St Saviour's and that included the renovation of the garden.

Maintenance of the garden, not surprisingly, continues to be an ongoing concern. Mention must be made though of the massive input of two late members of the Church who in their later years, though battling with the effects of aging and ill-health, were determined to keep going with the garden for as long as possible. Gardening was just one of many Church activities that Iris Head undertook with such dedication. Another member has said, 'If I was looking for Iris, I could be almost sure to find her in the Church garden.' Roy Graham was a church warden for some years. He was passionate about gardening and would regularly transport his mower to cut the grass at the Church. He also had his own allotment. Iris and Roy both died in 2017.

Group Activities at the Church

This part of the story of St Saviour's, old and new, looks at some of the group activities, those making use of the Church hall and rooms and group activities within the Church. Included are group activities which supported fitness or sports; that represented specific organisations; for different age groups or social needs and those focussing on spiritual learning and development. All represent aspects of the Church's ministry. What comes over clearly is that across many decades the Church is very much a centre of activity, social as well as religious, in the community in a way that is far less evident today. There were also aspects of health and social support which were not necessarily available in other forms at the time. But the coming and going of different activities also highlight other changes which impacted on the Church's relationship with its community.

The Jubilee booklet of 1934 celebrating the original St Saviour's underlines that the Church was active in supporting the social side of local life and lists an amazing array – badminton, cricket, football, tennis, swimming, rambling and cycling clubs, gymnasium, debating societies, lantern lectures, Temperance, Band of Hope, Scouts and Guides – all of which 'contributed a worthy part in the progress of the Church' (Woods 1934, p.35). Going back even earlier we see in the few parish magazines that still exist for the years 1904 to 1923 references to many different groups reflecting both spiritual and social activities and activities expected of the church at that time. For example in the parish magazine for September 1907 under the heading 'Parochial Organisations' are listed: Communicants Union; Ladies Missionary Working Party; Men's Missionary Band; C.M.S Gleaner's Union; Band of Hope; St Saviour's Temperance Society; Scripture Union; Sowers' Band; Ladies Working Party; Mission to Lepers; Mothers' Meetings;

Men's Services; Young Men's Institute; Choral Society; Cycling Club; Football Club.

Temperance groups and meetings were a common feature of churches in the 19th and early 20th century campaigning against alcohol and promoting total abstinence. The Band of Hope was founded in Leeds in 1847 as a group which aimed specifically to dissuade children from drinking alcohol. In a local newspaper there is an article about the first annual meeting of St Saviour's branch of the Church of England Temperance Society in 1888 presided over by Rev. Henderson Burnside. Unfortunately it records that 'there were very few people present' (Stratford Express 1888b, p.3).

The Original Church Hall

Tantalisingly there is often little detail in minutes of parish meetings. We have to make the most of snippets of information and comments, and the all-important memories of Church members. Together these help to create a picture of what was happening at the Church and the use made of the Church and its hall. For part of the period we are focussing on, the church hall in Macdonald Road was a building separate to the Church which fronted Station Road. A range of groups met in and used the church halls. The hall building then consisted of two halls, the main and 'small' hall as it was called, and it was much smaller. The main hall had a large stage/platform. Key activities at this time were:

Gymnasium

One activity that is regularly highlighted is that of a gymnasium. It was an important feature in the early life of the church hall. An item from the November 1906 parish magazine refers to the St Saviour's Institute and Gymnasium being 'in full swing' by the time the article would be printed. In the May 1907 magazine under the heading 'Well done Gymnasium!' congratulations are offered for the 'grand display given by the combined members, Ladies and Gentlemen'. A letter of 1936 listing activities also includes both a boys and girls gymnasium. A record of October

1958 records the start of gymnasium classes for boys and girls. In December 1958 Christian Endeavour, having been offered a climbing rope, ask if it can be fitted to the apex of the roof. Lutons (the firm regularly helping the Church out with building issues at this time) fit the rope accordingly. Church member Ray Vincent recalls the boys gym club, 'All the usual apparatus seen in a gymnasium was available in the hall. It is still possible to see where the anchor points in the floor were for some of the apparatus'.

Uniformed Groups

Ray also recalls the uniformed groups which included Brownies Cubs, Guides and Scouts meeting in the halls once a week. In December 1954 in an item about the heating of the hall it is stated that Guides used the hall on Mondays, Cubs on Wednesdays and Brownies on Fridays. The Cub pack was only for members of the Sunday school.

Over the years we come across more references to the Scouts in particular. They were the 24th West Ham Group:

4th April 1957 : The Scouts to pay £2 per annum for use of church hall.

19th August 1960 : There is a complaint about noise from the church hall at 11.45pm on Monday 8 August 1960, and the Secretary is asked to write to the group Scout Master to ask for an explanation.

12th February 1962: The group scoutmaster (Mr Falloway) requests exclusive use of the classroom which is at present also being used as a store room. The group would be prepared to redecorate and install supplementary heating. It would be used by the Scouts as a 'den' but other organisations could arrange to use it. 'After a very wide discussion it was agreed' the room would be cleared but there must be a leader for any organisation using the room. But it took over a year before all parties were satisfied with the conditions.

1st April 1963: The vicar spoke of his meeting with the scouts and scout master about non-attendance of scouts at church services or Sunday school and stated that if not prepared to fulfil this obligation as a controlled group, he would have to close it down. He was supported by the District Scoutmaster in this. The outcome is that members started attending church. The Group had been awarded the Queen's Scouts Badge so as well as the ticking off about church attendance, congratulations were also due.

28th October 1963: We hear that the Scouts have now transferred to Durning Hall and the Cubs have also had to transfer. The Senior Scouts had already moved to Norwich Road Congregational Church. 'The 24th West Ham Group had therefore been closed'.

A parish magazine that survives for October 1965 refers to a Guide Company meeting on Mondays at 7.15pm and a Brownie Pack meeting on Wednesdays at 6pm. It is popular and there are no vacancies at that point. In 1969 though, the Guide Company closed. In February 1967 we read that organisations using the hall were not charged a set rent, 'leaders of each group to be left to give as they feel led'.

Groups within the Church

Sunday Schools

Ray Vincent remembers the time when the Sunday school met at 3pm. There was a group for very young children in the small room at the front of the church. The next age group met in the small hall in several classes and in the main hall there were five classes for girls and five for boys. The older teenagers met in the large room in the vicarage also on a Sunday afternoon.

It had long been the custom to hold Sunday school separately to the services and looking back in the archives it is interesting to note what was expected. We read in the parish magazine of September 1917 under the heading 'Sunday School Lessons', 'parents are specially requested that their children attend school regularly, punctually, bring their books, learn the Texts, and to see that the attendance card has been stamped Early or Late'! The texts to be studied were announced a month ahead.

Over the decades at St Saviour's, it was also customary most years for the Sunday school teachers to run an outing for the children and their families These outings were a long-held tradition and much valued especially in times when few parents had their own cars. The venues included Chalkwell (near Southend). The Church hired carriages on the train from Wanstead Park Station. Ray recalls that in alternate years the Sunday school went to Theydon Bois by coach and enjoyed a day in Epping Forest with tea provided by the local church in their hall.

The parish magazines tell us about some Sunday school outings in the early decades of the 20th century. For example in June 1906 we read of a Sunday school excursion by special train to Dovercourt. The party numbered exactly 300, the largest for some years. In 1916 a party of over 220 adults and children took a trip to Theydon Bois. It was noted that it was the twentieth year in succession that St Saviour's had a fine day for the Sunday school excursion. In June 1920 a party of 350 took a special train from Wanstead Park to Southend.

Jean Murphy, herself a Sunday school teacher at St Saviour's for 30 years, describes some of the general changes in how and when Sunday Schools are run:

'In earlier decades the Sunday schools were always very well attended. Even though the parents might not come to church nevertheless they made sure their children went to Sunday school which was normally held in the afternoon. When Sunday Schools ceased to be separate post-service or Sunday afternoon activities, at a certain point in the service the young people left for their own lessons. Kings Club for children 4-11 years in the church hall, and Pathfinders from 11-15 years into the Pathfinders Room, and this is the system in place now. These days the children and young people are usually from churchgoing families. Numbers have fluctuated over the decades with cultural changes and the decrease in Christian influence.'

Jean, though, remembers high attendance even in the late 1980s. The AGM of 13th April 1987 records an increase of children at Sunday school 'more than ever before' with an average of 20 children. And a comment from the AGM of 10th April 1989 which is echoed today is the call for more helpers in Sunday school and Pathfinders so that the same people are not missing the service each time.

Fluctuations in attendance were not necessarily just a recent occurrence. At the meeting on 27th September 1966 the vicar (then John Williams) spoke of concern around the decline of Sunday school numbers and efforts to ascertain from parents the best timing. There had been general approval to combine Sunday school as part of the Family Service at 10.30 for about half an hour of class teaching in hall. Perhaps this was the start of the Sunday school activities being undertaken simultaneously with the morning service.

King's Club

The Sunday school for younger children became known as the King's Club and has benefited from the input and dedication of a goodly number of church members over the decades. Past teachers include: Betty Osborne, Iris Head, Glynis Scarborough, Jean Rough, Nellie Cox, Jean Murphy, Margaret Jupp, Jean Dunhill, Mrs. Hanchard, Miss Rackham, Violet Wedge, Mrs Currie, and Jocelyn Brown.

Recollections of long-serving teachers

Jean Murphy describes the kind of sessions that were run during the 30 years she helped with the King's Club in the 'new' St Saviour's using the small hall and various rooms within the Church. The programme consisted in singing choruses, prayers and a fun game related to the Bible story they were about to hear. There were three age groups in Kings Club and after the game the members would then go to their particular age group for the Bible story and activity leaflets. Many of the materials were provided by the Scripture Union. As continues today, on Communion Sundays, both the King's Club members and the Pathfinders rejoin the congregation for Communion or for a blessing at the Communion rail before returning to their group sessions.

Andy Spraggs remembers being taught by Jean, and Miriam Gordon and her sister Leah remember being taught well in King's Club by the various teachers whose personalities complemented each other. The special prayers said for the children and for the young people attending Pathfinders have a particular resonance for Miriam who feels that, 'the prayers for the young people to walk with God have been answered in part as I continue my journey with Him.'

Two other long-serving leaders of the group are Emily Kirton and Glenys Gordon. By the time of writing this in 2022, they have both been involved for 40 years. Over that period of time they have taught the children and the grandchildren of various Church members. Emily recalling her early involvement looks back at how they became involved:

> Glenys and I began teaching the three-and-a-half-year to six- year-olds, the seven-to- eight-year-olds were taught by Jean Murphy. When Iris and Glynis left, due to other commitments, it was Glenys, Jean Murphy, Margaret Jupp, and I and we had to split the classes in two with Glenys and I teaching the younger age group up to age seven and Margaret and Jean taking the eight-to-eleven-year-olds.

In busier times they had to make good use of whatever space was available: 'it's hard to think that we had four teaching spaces full of young people.' The room opposite the vestry was used by Jean Rough for the younger age group. Jean Murphy was in the smaller hall area and Iris, Glynis, Glenys and Emily shared the main hall, end to end. Parents were able to take their babies to the crèche room and still listen to the service as there was a speaker in there. A Sunday school notice board had a sheet for each child where they put their star stickers to record their attendance. Once the sheet was completed they would be given a little gift and a new sheet would be started. For young people a Bible was also presented at the end of the year for regular attendance.

Emily and Glenys remember the training sessions which were held on Saturdays once every three months in a church in Leyton. These sessions were for all local Sunday school teachers enabling them to meet each other. They were able to help one another through discussions on resources used, and methods and formats they could apply in teaching and in helping different age groups to understand the Bible.

Numbers attending have varied considerable over the years but currently (2022) there is a very enthusiastic group of children and young people

Other key helpers over more recent years have been and are: Rebecca Akinsanmi; Angela Bannister; Pauline Bookal-Downes; Hillary Henry; Jackie Thomas; Dorothea Britten.

Younger People's Groups

Ray Vincent recalls that in the 1960s there were youth clubs for two age-ranges. The first club was set up for late teens and early twenties. As a result of the popularity of this club the younger members of the church demanded a group of their own which was formed and met on a Saturday evening. There was an after church young people's group, and a thriving choir. The older teens and early twenties age-group, known as Crossfire, met after the Sunday Evening Service to quiz the vicar, John Williams, and 'unpick the sermons', and also present was Betty Osborne, the parish worker – 'discussions went on well into the evening.' The Sunday evening service was at this time the main service. The group also enjoyed a number of self-catering summer holidays together starting in 1968 when the group borrowed a minibus to drive to the far end of Cornwall where they spent a week looking after themselves in 'glorious Gorran Haven'. This led to further holidays in the Lake District, North Wales and Somerset.

In the parish magazine that exists for October 1965, Reverend John Williams describes a mid-week meeting for all boys and girls between the ages of eight and twelve called Christian Endeavour. Meeting on Thursday evenings at 6.15pm the group came together 'to sing choruses, receive simple Bible training and play games'. John adds, 'We are hoping to start a junior department for those between five and seven'. That month also saw the start of a group for older young people in the form of a games evening closing with an Epilogue. Jean Murphy recalls, 'during the 1960s and 1970s there was an Explorers group which was open to children from 8 to 11 years and held on Thursday evenings. This was led by our lady worker Betty Osborne ably assisted by Mrs. Coulson who was a member of the congregation. The evening consisted of fun games and a

Bible lesson.' The PCC AGM for 12th April 1983 refers to Young People's Fellowship starting around this time.

In the mid 1990s Beryl Duggan and Angela Hill, and other adult helpers, ran a youth club for ages 11-16. The club was very popular with around 40 young people attending every week. Ambrose Gordon recalls that some of the boys attending won a trophy at a football tournament. In September 1999 the need for a youth worker was raised and Bola Adamolekum was appointed and took over the running of the club. The AGM held in April 2001 refers to a new Wednesday girl's group called E-Mission. Some other memories that Ambrose has is Bola organising a young people sleep over in the Church hall and Pathfinder room, and Walter and Jean Tee organising a couple of walks/hikes around Docklands and Essex.

Pathfinders

A group named Pathfinders which is now held alongside the Sunday service and caters for young people, seems to have been in existence since the late 1960s or early 1970s. Discussions, games and other activities based on Bible readings, material from the Scripture Union 'GRID Light' programme and many other resources that the teachers bring to the meetings, aim to help young Christians deal with the challenges of modern society and to grow spiritually. Activities include discussions, talks on specific topics, Bible reading, games and quizzes. The age group attending is 10 to 15 year olds but in the 2017 annual report it is recorded that older teens are able to stay on in the group, as there is no other group. As leader Ambrose Gordon writes, 'this means that the Pathfinder leaders have to try and plan a programme for an increasingly wider age range i.e. a child who is just leaving primary school to a young person about to go to college or university'. He adds 'it is a challenge but I am sure that with plenty of prayer and support we can do it'.

Ambrose himself is recorded at the AGM of 21st April 1988 as having joined Andrew Coulson to help with Pathfinders. And for many years Ambrose ran Pathfinders on his own, which was challenging because he was also a Scout leader at the 2nd Newham (Busby) Scout Group. There were times when Pathfinders group did not meet because he was away camping or on other Scout activities.

Over a period of time Ambrose had support from Beryl Duggan and Jenny Somers. At the PCC meeting of 4th December 1995 it is recorded that 'Beryl Duggan has offered to help Ambrose with Pathfinders'. Ambrose remembers that Beryl had a particular gift for planning and organising the church services led by the children and young people, such as Christingle, Harvest and Mothering Sunday. Leah Gordon recalls when she and her sister attended Pathfinders the teachers were her father Ambrose, Jenny, Beryl, and Joyce Lindsay. She has a particularly fond memory of Joyce starting each session with a Psalm and encouraging the group to read Psalms on a daily basis, and as a result Leah has continued to read Psalms regularly. Leah's sister Miriam remembers Joyce suggesting that they read and try and memorise the Psalm equivalent to their age, and she recalls Joyce as a very engaging and passionate leader in Pathfinders. She also remembers being taught by Beryl and how good she was at coming up with new ideas in her teaching and getting the young people to participate. And she remembers the wise insights from Milton Watson who helped out at times.

In the 1990 AGM minutes a regular attendance at Pathfinders of 9-10 is recorded. Ten year later numbers were rising and with the arrival of a youth worker, Bola Adamolekum in 2010, Pathfinders was divided up and a new first stage group formed known as The Next Dimension. In 1996 there is a report on a Pathfinders 'Games Evening' to be held on a Thursday. There were 13 in attendance at the first meeting including several who were not members of the regular Pathfinders group.

There are comments in reports and minutes on the need for more help and by 2018/19 Ambrose and long-term helper Jenny Somers are aiming to take more of a back seat as other Church members and younger members become more involved in teaching, as well as youth workers appointed by the Forest Gate Churches Youth Project. Over the many years Ambrose has been running the group other Church members who have helped out have been: Rebecca Akinsanmi; Elizabeth Akinsanmi; Amy Lindsay; Joyce Lindsay; Andrew Lindsay; Milton Watson; Melissa Watson; Doreen Alexander; Noel Brown; Jenny Somers; Angela Hill; Beryl Duggan; Chris Ogbeifun; Sophia Kusi; Tosin Agbaje.

Chris, who in his twenty years at St Saviour's, has also served as treasurer, assistant church warden and is on the PCC, is thankful to God for enabling him to perform these roles, especially that of treasurer.

Some of the younger Church members, including Leah and Miriam as well as Melissa, who have grown up attending the King's Club and Pathfinder groups and are now helping to run them, are also developing a new group and new activities for younger people. A current development from a Friday evening Bible Study organised by the Rev. Henry, is a group for those aged 18 to 35, Young Christians Together, who meet regularly at the Church for 'faith, food, friendship and fun'.

Youth workers are and have been an important staffing element within the Church though funding opportunities have been limited. Bola who became youth worker at a time when there many young people involved in the activities was possibly funded by the Oasis Trust. The AGM of 2006 states that youth workers from seven different churches in the area are meeting monthly. In recent years, since 2017, there have been two appointments in the role of a youth worker to work across three churches, Emmanuel, All Saints and St Saviour's. Due to lack of funding, these have been much appreciated but temporary posts.

Children's and Young People's Services

For specific celebrations the children often undertake craftwork such as making cards and pictures, using resources provided by the teachers. This results in wonderful displays of colourful designs for Christmas (Christingle), and Harvest Festival, and for Mother's and Father's Days. These services are planned and led by the children, young people and their teachers.

On these and other occasions King's Club and Pathfinders also join forces to plan and carry out the content for these services in very creative and thoughtful ways. This includes readings, leading prayers, mini-dramas, singing both choral and solo, dancing and performances on instruments including piano and ukulele.

Some of the younger members of the Church also participate in doing the Readings during the regular services.

Elite Kids Club

Another dimension for some years now has been the use of the Church hall for a breakfast club, after school club and holiday club, The Elite Kids Club, run by church member Sophia Kusi. Although not directly a Church group there are actual and potential mutual benefits in its close relationship with the Church, and Sophia sees it as a ministry to the children in the community.

Bible Study, Praise and Prayer

Jean Murphy recalls, 'every week there was a Bible Study group called Tuesday Link as well as Praise and Prayer on Friday evenings.' She also recalls that a Bible Study on Wednesday was led by Betty Osborne as a Home Group which met at Mrs Coulson's flat .Whilst on Thursdays there was a Bible Study group at the Rectory. These are both mentioned in AGM minutes for 30th April 1990 which also refers to a young people's Bible Study on Monday evenings.

Pauline Haywood, who was later to become a church warden, recalls, 'I started to attend the Bible study group on a Wednesday evening, led by the Rev. John Williams, sharing information understanding the Bible, I knew this was what was missing in my life, and that St Saviours was going to be a part of me.' Further on, the Wednesday Bible Study was led by Pat Vincent at the Rectory and it is mentioned that Pat reports on this group at the 11th April 2010 AGM.

The AGM minutes of 29th April 1981 comment that, 'Praise and Prayer meetings continue to be important and they average about 25 meeting together for prayer'.

The Monday evening Bible Study Group which was started in November 1999 was initially led by Ann Turner, and then by Grace Ani. The group used study guides from the Scripture Union and other Christian publishers. In the AGM reports Grace has often provided a summary of what has been studied through the year.

In the annual report for 2014 membership is fairly constant at 10 to 12 members, all women, though it is not intended for women only, and in 2017 the membership is 11 in number. Ann reports that on the second Monday of alternate months, the Group, along with other women from St Saviour's and other local churches, have been attending the face-to-face meetings at All Saints, Woodford Wells. These are evangelistic meetings for women with guest speakers, testimonies, worship and prayer. This attendance came to an end when numbers reduced and there were problems with transportation

During the Covid-19 pandemic, because meetings were not allowed, an online Bible Study and prayer group was organised by the Rev. Henry and this group continues to meet online via Zoom on Tuesday evenings.

Banner-Making Group

This group came about in the late seventies when ideas for Lent workshops were being explored. One idea for a workshop was a banner making group, an idea not welcomed by some members of the Church. But the group carried on and two Easter banners were produced during the first Lent course. The resistance to banners melted away when the church members saw what the group had produced. The ministry of the banners is now a vital part of St Saviour's as well as giving glory to God.

The banners provide a wonderful alternative to stained glass windows and do much to enliven the Church environment. St Saviour's does not have any stained glass windows, though it has plenty of windows and is a very light and often sun-filled Church. Stained glass windows also serve as an informative illustration of a Biblical story or text. The banners, however, are an equally good witness to the Bible's teachings, providing visual and memorable learning by highlighting and illustrating key texts, with the added advantage of regular changing of banners according to the time of the Church year. Indeed their portability also proved an advantage in 2020 when lockdown during the Covid-19 pandemic closed all churches. The vicar was able to take some banners to the Rectory to be used as part of the Sunday services streamed from there on Facebook and YouTube.

In the 2016 AGM report Pat Vincent, as main organiser, describes how the group often works. The group meets on an irregular basis as work is also done by its members in their spare time at home. When the group does meet it is usually at Pat's home where fellowship, laughter and Ray's home-baked cake or cheese scones are enjoyed. Over the years the collection of banners has grown considerably. At the AGM of April 2017 it was noted that there were 65 banners and of course many more have been done since. Some of the original banners have been refurbished now that experience over the years has improved techniques and established a 'house style'. Banners have also been made for individuals to hang at home, and have travelled far, taken by members of the congregation to Pakistan, Nigeria and three islands in the Caribbean.

Women's and Men's Fellowships

A rare copy of an older parish magazine that exists for October 1965 refers to a number of groups: the Young Wives Group meeting twice a month at 8pm on a Monday 'to "knit and natter" over a cup of tea and to join in the Epilogue'; and the Women's Fellowship meeting every Thursday at 3pm. The 1981 AGM minutes mentions that there were usually more than 20 women attending the Fellowship. By the 1987 AGM numbers attending averaged nine.

Jean Murphy recalls the Ladies Meetings held during the 1980s. These took place in a room in Bacchus's Bin, a bar at Maryland Point, just on the edge of Stratford and each time a speaker would be invited. The organiser was Mervis Allen who for some years was also a church warden at St Saviour's, alongside Ken Jupp. The more neutral surroundings encouraged others to come who might not feel so comfortable attending in a church, and numbers increased. 'It was a warm welcoming and multi-cultural group and proved to be a wonderful vehicle of evangelism.'

In 2019, at the suggestion of church members and led by Grace Ani, a new Women's Fellowship was formed with the aims of providing an additional supportive, caring and nurturing network across the church community. A further aim was to develop outreach opportunities, connecting with the local community through other women's groups. Aims and objectives were established and welfare and prayer teams set up. The group, which met after services on the first Sunday of the month, was just getting into its stride when the Covid-19 pandemic struck. Although meetings came to a halt, the Fellowship helped to provide a structure for keeping in touch at a distance, and particularly with more isolated and vulnerable members.

At various times there have been men's groups and they were very prevalent in the earlier years of the Church. In more recent decades a Men's Fellowship met at the Railway Tavern in Forest Gate. Albert Gordon remembers being part of the Men's

Fellowship. About six of them would regularly gather together fairly informally over a drink. Rev. John Williams would encourage them to share testimonies. The DCC meeting for 13th September 1993 refers to a men's meeting at Railway Tavern which has to change venue due to new management at the Tavern. Because of the success of Bacchus's Bin as a venue, the men's group moved there.

Community Outreach Activities

Often groups that developed were partly a response to a social need and were outreach activities encouraging members of the local community to make use of the Church, and hopefully participate also in its spiritual activities.

Parent / Carer, Baby and Toddler Group

There was obviously a growing need for a group. Meetings of March and June 1991 refer to a group of child minders who want to use the church hall once a fortnight and there are discussions about purchasing toys. The need for a Mother and Toddler Group was raised specifically at a meeting in October 1991 and it was suggested by Päivi Takala that it be run once a week. Päivi was one of the members of the Finnish Lutheran Mission commissioned to work with the growing Asian population in Forest Gate – more about this in a later section.

The group met on Wednesday mornings during term time from 9.30am to midday. Church member Ann Turner was enrolled early on to help out at a time when she had her own two-year old toddler. Ann has provided many of the details included here. She writes that there were 'many lovely willing helpers' which included mums from Odessa School. Church member Pauline Haywood remembers that she first heard about St Saviours Church when she was approached outside the Odessa School Nursery by Ann who was telling the mums about the mother and toddler group. 'I went with my friend. The group was very friendly and welcoming.' Pauline later helped with the group and other Church members regularly involved were Jean Murphy, Jenny Somers and Georgina Leadeham.

The group was very popular and both Ann and Jean recall the diversity of the group, in race, religion and gender. As well as mums, there were sometimes dads, grandmas and occasionally grandads. And sometimes childminders brought their charges. A Sikh family regularly attended as a result of Päivi's contact with Asian families in the community, and other religions were represented. Ann writes, 'everyone got along really well and we celebrated all the Christian festivals, and at times of their festivals, parents of other faiths would bring their special foods as treats at break time.'

The group inherited many toys from the previous Childminders Group which by then had ceased to run. There were lots of activities which were varied regularly but included a 'messy' activity every week which might be sand or water play, painting or print-making. There were singing sessions and a quiet corner with books and jigsaws. And there was a much-needed break time when everyone could wind down from all the activities. In summer an outing was usually organised, often to one of the local parks or Wanstead Flats, and visits were made to the City Farm in Leyton.

Ann applied for a grant from Newham Council which was used to buy more toys and some cupboards for storage. The group was then assigned an Early Years Worker by the Council and she visited once or twice a term providing useful advice and information. This was Sue Fisher who later began attending St Saviour's regularly and, with Ann, started the Wednesday Welcome. As far as possible the group was self-funding and the Church facilities were provided free of charge. A charge of 50p per adult was made, irrespective of number of children brought along. This also covered some refreshment. In addition a whole range of fund-raising activities added to the kitty. One of these was rental of videos for a small charge. There were also coffee mornings which sometimes included craft and book stalls and children's clothes made by parents, and cards and gifts at Christmas – a share of profits being donated to the fund. A very popular money-raising activity was visits from a professional photographer, Dave Bonnington. These usually took place on a Saturday as part of coffee mornings and were open also to families who were not attending the group

Parents and carers were encouraged to attend Harvest and Christmas services, and a number did. Jean recalls, 'this led in later years to "Come On and Celebrate" which was held on the last Sunday evening in each month and was an informal time of worship where it was easier to invite non-churchgoers to come and get to know members of the congregation.'

The Group was asked to be involved with a parenting course for parents of young children that had been developed by the church in Northern Ireland. Mums and carers from other local churches were also involved. The meetings were organised by Jenny Sainsbury, wife of the then Bishop of Barking Roger Sainsbury, and were held at St Saviour's either in the Pathfinder or crèche room with about 10 to 12 attending. Different aspects of parenting were discussed over about 12 sessions. The aim was to assess the course and see whether it was worth promoting for wider use across the Diocese.

St Saviour's Parent/Carer and Toddler Group ran for 10 years stopping in 2001 as numbers dropped. In the1990s it had been a response to a very definite need but over the 10 years there were marked changes socially. More mums were returning to work and some workplaces were providing crèches and nursery facilities. There was more government provision of early years childcare and many more private nursery places were becoming available.

Open House

During the 1970's, and possibly to build on the interest created by the commencement of worship and activities at the new St Saviour's, an initiative known as Open House began. It was essentially a social activity enabling people to spend time away from their homes and enjoy company, activities and food together. But it also had possibilities for attracting newcomers to the Church. Jean Murphy recalls:

> In 1978 Open House was started by our lady worker, Betty Osborne. It was held every Wednesday between 11am and 4pm.

It gave church members the opportunity to invite friends and neighbours to relax with others in a non-threatening atmosphere. Tea, coffee and then a light meal were provided by church members. Through Open House a number of people started coming to our special services such as at Christmas and Harvest, etc. A few went on to become regular members of our congregation. Open House continued until 1985.

Minutes of October 1978 record that Open House had commenced with 'some success achieved'. The AGM minutes of April 1979 record that an average of 15 people were attending each week and describe the initiative as 'a bridge to the outsider'. April 1981 records attendance as being about 20. The AGM of 1983 reported that over the four years since it started 47 individuals had attended Open House, of which 19 had no previous connection with the Church and that this has 'brought some families into the Church'. By April 1985 we learn that Open House now runs from 1.30pm to 4pm.

Wednesday Welcome

In similar vein to Open House, in 2015 Wednesday Welcome was commenced at the Church by two members, Ann Turner and Sue Fisher, with regular help from other members, especially Maxine Morris. Sessions were held fortnightly from 1.30pm to about 3.30pm with the aim of providing a social afternoon aimed particularly at older people as an opportunity to get out and socialise. A chance to chat while carrying out activities such as colouring, craft work, knitting, quizzes, was followed by tea, coffee and cakes served invitingly on tables in the small hall. Knitting and crocheting activities within the Church directly contributed to the Church's offering to Operation Christmas Child. In the annual report of 2016 attendance was reported as being between eight and sixteen people, depending on the weather. Although most attending were Church members, relatives and friends joined in as well. In 2017 a special outing was arranged to a local Café 'Lakeside Café' in Cann Hall Road. The Covid-19 pandemic has prevented the continuation of Wednesday Welcome for the time being.

Food Bank

Poverty of course is not confined to any one era but there are times when it becomes more evident. The financial crisis of 2007-2008 and subsequent recession, then followed by a government policy of austerity helped to create a situation in which, even though employment levels improved, salaries did not keep pace with rising costs of living. At the same time with the introduction of Universal Credit, benefits in some cases were reduced or often made harder to apply for. In London poverty is highlighted even more by the considerable gap between those with wealth and those on lower incomes. In response to this there has been a rapid growth in the provision of food banks to provide some extra support to individuals and families in getting sufficient food on the table. St Saviour's food bank opened in 2013/14 as a development from the Harvest Festival celebration when, for many years, food contributed has been shared with a local charity. The food bank is stocked by Church members and others including contributions from a nearby store, one of two remaining shops in Station Road. At the Harvest Festival the extra food gathered, including contributions from the local St James' Church of England Junior School, is also shared with the Refugee and Migrant Project (RAMP) in Newham. It is seen as a vital part of the Church's community outreach.

In 2022 we are facing a cost of living crisis the likes of which has not been seen for decades. All sorts of factors have interplayed to bring this about including the impact of the Covid-19 pandemic, effects of leaving the European Union, the devastating conflict between Russia and the Ukraine, and rapidly increasing energy prices. 'Heating or eating' has become a much used phrase underlining the difficult choices many may have to make. Demands on food banks nationwide are growing while at the same time there are less people able to contribute. The reliance upon this help is reflected in the growing number of food banks or food pantries that have now opened up in the local area – Woodgrange Baptist Church, Emmanuel Church, The Magpie Project and St Margaret's Church Leytonstone.

Social Events over the Decades

Social events are interpreted widely to include fellowship events which are part social but are also opportunities for sharing, learning, spiritual and developmental activities, as well as events to raise money and entertain, and to involve and attract the wider community. Inevitably this is just a selection of events that were well documented and represent different decades.

In the 1950s and 1960s regular events were garden fetes, jumble sales and special teas. For example, at a meeting of 8th February 1954, it was proposed that a garden party be held on 12th June, 'this is to be larger than in the past and include extra stalls and an entertainment and sideshows'. A 'missionary garden party' was held in July 1963. In 1953 a jumble sale was organised specifically to raise money for improvements in the hall kitchen. In the late 1950's Reverend and Mrs Hampton organised 'Daffodil' and 'Chrysanthemum' Teas at the appropriate time of the year. These are just examples of many events held.

The Annual Bazaar

One event that does stand out in records is the annual bazaar. This seems to have been an event of some long-standing as references to a bazaar appear in parish magazines that exist for the early 1900s. But certainly it is notable that this event, by the 1950s, and usually held in November, dominates in terms of planning and organisation. This is evidenced by the amount of mentions and space given to bazaar preparations in the hand-written PCC minutes. For example at a meeting on 1st October 1954 a whole page is dedicated to bazaar preparations. As well as the bazaar itself one or more jumble sales were held during the year to raise money for the running of the bazaar and help the stallholders participating. The 1953-4 annual report describes the bazaar as 'an unqualified success' with the mayor and mayoress of West Ham in attendance. At the meeting of 1st May 1956 there was a proposal to have 150-200 admission programmes. This gives some indication of the popularity of the bazaar locally. It is recorded that at the 1961 bazaar 355 people paid for admission. As well as the bazaar, much emphasis is placed on the quality of the concert following it. In 1957 we learn that a choir or group of singers named The Philomels are to give the concert again, and they are back to do the same in 1958.

The bazaar must have drawn a lot of people from the community to the Church, but how many became regular attendees remains unknown. What is also significant is the amount of money raised by the bazaar. The gross takings for the bazaar of 1955 were £215, 1 shilling and 2 pence. In 1956 it made £256, 8 shillings and 5 pence, and in 1959 made over £273. These were substantial sums. Figures were not always that high but remained fairly steady into the sixties.

When Canon John Williams became vicar in 1965 it is evident that increasingly he is uncomfortable with the holding of a bazaar and jumble sales to raise money for the Church, and he proposes as an alternative a system of 'direct giving'. The jumble sales for 1966 are dropped. There is a suggestion of considerable discussions around proposals but finally there is agreement on a Gift Day and a social gathering in November 1967. The bazaar is no more.

Parish House Parties

Ray Vincent recalls that the 1970s marked a major change in the way the Church was run. With Canon John Williams as the rector it was the start of a number of social and fellowship activities. Remembered fondly are the house parties and weekend gatherings which combined leisure activities with worship and Bible study. Ray thinks that the week-long house parties were inspired by the success of the holiday weeks that the young people's group had started in 1968. By the seventies, Ray comments: 'It was clear that the rest of the congregation wanted to get in on the act as they learnt what a good time the young people were having.'

So this led to a Parish House Party being held at Cromer in August 1972. It was a significant event for Jean Murphy who recalls:

> I was an active member of my local church but was becoming more interested in the activities at St Saviour's... In 1972 the Rev. John Williams and the lady worker Betty Osborne organised the first house party which took place at a Christian Alliance Guest House in Cromer, Norfolk. My friends invited me to the house party and during that week I got to know other members of the congregation and joined them in the leisure activities during the day and the worship and Bible Study in the evenings. That week was a spiritual turning point in my life. Although I had always believed in God, through John and Betty's ministry I was introduced to the work and Person of the Holy Spirit in my life. It was almost as if the blinkers had been removed from my eyes and a whole new spiritual vista had opened up for me.

The success of the Cromer house party led to others being held over the next ten years or so in various seaside towns including Cliftonville, Ilfracombe, Westbrook, Felixstowe, Hastings, Swanage and Sheringham. The most popular venues were Westbrook (near Margate) and Sheringham and a number of return visits were made to these towns. Private or Christian Alliance guest houses and small hotels were used. The format was that each morning after breakfast the group would meet together in the lounge for a time of prayer and worship. After that some would go for walks, or into town or onto the beach to relax in the sun or play ball games. In the evening, after dinner, the group met together in the lounge for a time of worship and Bible study. It was customary that on one day during the week group members would pile into whatever cars were available to visit a nearby place of interest. Ray summarises the overall impact of the house parties as, 'invaluable occasions' which 'helped to build fellowship with one another and moved us forward spiritually.' The house parties also inspired a monthly renewal meeting, 'Trinity Renewal'.

Away Days and Weekend Breaks

Ray describes these as being dedicated to study. Venues included Wetheringsett Manor, Chigwell, Battle and Mulberry House in Ongar, Essex. In the minutes of 31st March 1970 there is reference to a parish weekend 'Springboard' to be held at Chesham Bois in April of that year. In 1989 an autumn weekend was organised at Wetheringsett. Change comes in the 1990s. The minutes of a meeting in March 1993 notes that there is less interest in parish weekends and, by this time, Wetheringsett was now organised for self-catering which was less appropriate.

Day Trips and Trips Abroad

A day outing in summer continues to be an annual event at the Church often to a seaside resort along the east and south coasts. Anne and Albert Gordon remember with fondness outings in previous decades, many of them organised by the then lady worker Betty Osborne. Everything was done as a group together with organised games and shared picnics. Recent outings organised by David Martins have been Westcliffe on Sea (2016), Weston-Super-Mare (2017), Broadstairs (2018), Hastings (2019). There was no summer outing in 2020 or 2021 due to the Covid-19 pandemic. Leah Gordon enjoyed trips to Hastings in particular but associates Great Yarmouth with rain and a trip there when she was eight or nine and was scared by heavy thunder. Despite the miserable weather on occasions, for Miriam Gordon these outings 'consolidated a love of the seaside, the sand and the sun (when it decided to come out!)'.

Mentions of day outings in the parish records surveyed are relatively few. Some that are mentioned over the decades are an outing to Chessington Zoo in 1974, to Southwold in 1989 and Walton-on-the-Naze in 1994. In the October 1965 parish magazine, one of few remaining ones, the Reverend John Williams writes, 'not often do you find a whole train full of church people, but you will if you happen to be at Forest Gate Station on Saturday October 30th at 8.29am. The reason? People from churches in all parts of Newham are joining together to go on a day's outing to see over some of the colleges of Cambridge and then to go on to Ely and worship at the Cathedral'.

But, for a period of time, there were also day trips abroad every other year. Trips remembered by Church members included Dunkirk, Boulogne, Bruges, St Omer and Le Touquet. Inevitably there were memorable episodes connected with some of these.

Jean Murphy and David Martins recall how on the return from a day trip to Le Touquet the coach was stopped by Passport Control. Rev John Williams got off to speak to an official and was told that the coach was radio-active! He got back on the coach and not wanting to panic anyone, laughingly asked, 'Is anyone on this coach radio-active?'. To which one lady who had come with friends from the church piped up, 'Yes, I am.' It appeared that she had received radiation treatment that week in hospital. Everyone else had to be checked out as well as the coach itself before all could get back on board. Then, because the drivers had worked their maximum hours, the coach had to wait at Medway services for replacements to arrive and it was about midnight before the coach got back to Forest Gate.

Leah enjoyed the day trips abroad because it was the first time she had been on a ferry. She and her sister Miriam remember with particular fondness a trip to Boulogne because the whole family went, including her grandparents, her aunt and uncle and cousin, and a family photo records the happy event.

There were also longer trips abroad. Ray Vincent says that these partly developed from the success of the week long house parties. Rev John Williams on five occasions led trips to Israel and once to Greece. Marie Spraggs remembers this trip to Greece as a pilgrimage in the footsteps of the Apostle Paul. Grace Ani went on four of the Israel trips in which they were joined by members of other churches and the local community in Forest Gate. Marie was amongst a group of people baptised in the River Jordan on one of these trips. Ray recalls a memorable first visit to Israel:

> In 1993 the Church broke new ground and organised a trip to Israel. By this time the whole of the Holy Land was open to visitors, so we were able to visit all the Bible sites without border problems. We approached Jerusalem from the Mount of Olives and it was easy to imagine Jesus coming down the hill and seeing the whole city laid out before him ... We soon realised why the New Testament writers talk about 'going up to Jerusalem'. The road we were travelling on to Jerusalem is one that approaches the city from the hills that surround it. The approach road up to the top of the hills is steep and winding and not very wide. In some places the coach was so long and the bends so sharp that the back end of the coach was overhanging the side of the cliff! Some of us were thankful which side of the coach we were seated.

The last Church trip to Israel was in 2009.

Other Social Events

Other social events regularly held over the decades were linked to Church festivals such as Easter social suppers and Harvest suppers. In 1965 and 1966 the Harvest suppers were followed by a film – *Touch of Brass* in 1965 and *Souls in Conflict* in 1966 – both linked with Evangelist Billy Graham who produced the latter. A Caribbean social evening was held in October 1991as part of an outreach programme for that year, and a Cockney social event was held in 1992. It is recorded that 108 people attended the Caribbean evening and raised a total of £130 towards the Church building fund. There are references to barn dances, barbecues in the rectory garden, and Ray Vincent recalls, 'Garden parties took place in the vicarage garden each year with games and other activities.' Jean Murphy also recalls that for some years a holiday club was held in August in the church hall and was always well attended. During the early 1960s there seems to have been a special connection with St Marks Church. A number of joint social activities hosted by both Churches are recorded in 1963 and 1964 and there is reference to a day visit to Coventry Cathedral organised by St Mark's. In recent years the popular event held in the rectory garden has been the fireworks party in November.

The Changing Social Context

Diversity and Racism

The 1960s through to the present day have seen considerable changes in the make-up of the population. This was noted by the Rev. John Williams who was vicar of St Saviour's from 1965 to 2012. He recalled that when he first came to St Saviours there was a largely white congregation. Over the years this started to change as first West Indians began coming to the UK, followed by people from various parts of Africa, then much later those from the Asian community and then Eastern Europeans. At the AGM of 10th April 1989, he remarked that it had been one of the most encouraging years since he started at St Saviour's both because of greater lay participation in worship and services and because the church was becoming more and more international. Today the congregation is mainly from the West Indian and African communities.

The attraction of Newham in the earlier decades was relatively cheap accommodation and job opportunities offered by companies such as the Dagenham Ford works, factories linked to the local docks and manufacturing industries. The E7 Now and Then website says that the 1981 census shows that 27% of Newham residents lived in a household headed by someone of 'New Commonwealth' background, about half of whom were Asian and a quarter Afro-Caribbean. At that time the Asian community was largely concentrated around East Ham and Upton Park, and Afro-Caribbean residents mainly centred in or around Forest Gate. Even back in the mid sixties there is some indication of the increasing internationality of the parish. The meeting for 27th April 1964 records that a request has been received from a gentleman in Essex Street to use the hall one evening a week for a devotional meeting for fellow West Indians and others. Permission was given for the hall to be used on Thursdays from 7.30-9.30pm.

But Newham was far from welcoming to many of its new inhabitants. The E7 Now and Then website describes the racial tensions of the 1970s and 1980s in Forest Gate. Racism was widespread and evident both in the community and within Newham Council, though some councillors did try to make a stand against this as did some organisations, Durning Hall in particular. For example, council housing policies were altered to avoid inclusion of Asian families and racist comments were openly made in the council and other meetings. Support for the National Front was also increasing. On 28th November 1977 the DCC report from St Matthew's refers to the racist activities of the National Front. The Rev. Williams suggests that the business meeting of the PCC be kept short so that time afterwards could be used to discuss other issues and he gave racial issues and spiritual issues as examples.

The PCC meeting of 19th April 1978 at St Saviour's records that action against racism would be taken up in the form of a petition. In the 1980s racially motivated attacks, murders and miscarriages of justice led to a big demonstration around the former Forest Gate police station in 1985 (E7 Now and Then 2018c).

In the minutes of March 1990 it states that Mr Udeozo is St Saviour's representative on the Newham Racial Equality Committee. Ako Udeozo who sadly died during the Covid-19 pandemic, continued in this role for many years.

Anne and Albert Gordon came over to England from St Vincent in the early sixties and were well aware of the racism of the times. In trying to find accommodation they often met with the, 'no coloureds, no Irish, no dogs' experience. When living in Mile End they had been deterred from attending church after being made to feel very unwelcome at a church in Roman Road. Instead they made the most of television programmes such as *Songs of Praise* which they much enjoyed.

They moved to Field Road in Forest Gate in 1966 and a neighbour, Mrs Armstrong, introduced them to St Saviour's. They remember that there were about four people of colour attending then. At their second visit, the vicar who took the service (John Williams newly appointed as vicar was taking more of an assistant role) made a point of talking to them and making them welcome. From then on they became very involved in Church life. Work sometimes meant they were unable to attend (Anne was an auxiliary nurse). Their neighbour would take one of their sons to Church. Their second son was baptised at St Saviour's. Anne remembers how important being a part of St Saviour's was to them in helping them to settle into a supportive community life. They remember how helpful and encouraging John Williams always was and the spirit of the Church was always a welcoming and caring one.

Albert became a sidesperson and remembers assisting church warden Ken Jupp sometimes as second signer of cheques. Albert and Roy Graham, who also lived in Field Road and was later to become church warden, helped out with a lot of tidying and maintenance tasks in the new St Saviour's and at the Rectory. The wooden free-standing cross by the altar at St Saviour's was one of two made by Albert. He got the wood from a yard in Cann Hall Road where wood reclaimed from buildings was sold. It was given to him for free when he told the owner what the wood was for.

The New Millennium

As with many organisations and activities the coming of the 21st century was an opportunity for churches to reflect and plan and consider social as well as faith issues. In advance an extensive questionnaire was circulated in the Diocese by the Bishop of Chelmsford as part of an initiative for 'Preparing the Church for the New Millennium'. A meeting of May 1999 attempted to summarise the responses provided by St Saviour's and refers to the changes in the community over the previous 25 years. The increase in Afro-Caribbean and Asian populations is noted but also increasing tolerance amongst different ethnic groups. The increase in numbers of refugees is also noted. Other social issues highlighted are: increase in single parents and social needs generally; less discipline in schools and at home; housing needs and drug issues. The responses also comment on significant changes in church flexibility and church experimentation with different patterns of services. As now there was a lot of change in the local population. Anne and Albert Gordon remember that a number of their friends and neighbours moved away, to areas perhaps where better educational, work and housing opportunities were offered.

Recent Social Issues

The issues referred to in the millennium document continue to present challenges to us as a Church and community and potentially could be further impacted by the current economic crisis and experiences of recent years. The Black Lives Matter movement has raised the profile of both historical and contemporary racist issues as has the 'Windrush scandal' in which government policy has discriminated against the first Caribbean immigrants and their children who came over on the *Windrush* ship in the 1950s and 60s. Many of these people never received a British passport and many of their children never received British citizenship despite being born here. Some were even unjustly deported back to various Caribbean islands from which they came legally many years prior.

The plight of refugees, asylum seekers and immigrants who are often escaping difficult, disadvantaged and often dangerous living situations remains a key issue. The Church offers some help to the Newham Refugees and Migrant Project (RAMP).

A more recent and alarming challenge is that of gang culture and in particular knife and gun crime affecting young people of colour in particular. Between 2003 and March 2021 there were 80 fatal stabbings in Newham (Falkner 2021). Some of these occurred in streets very local to the Church and some victims were known by members of the Church. Falkner's analysis shows a mix of factors that link to these homicides. An attempt to challenge this situation locally and constructively is Faith in Schools' project 'What's the Point?' which 'seeks to educate and empower young people to change the culture of youth violence' (Faith in Schools 2022). At time of writing Faith in Schools has run this project in a number of secondary schools in Newham and an early intervention version in three primary schools. Participants volunteer themselves and work in small groups of ten, taking an active lead. Gang members, victims of knife crime, and role models from different fields also take part.

Front of St Saviour's Church 2022

Side garden of St Saviour's and hall entrance

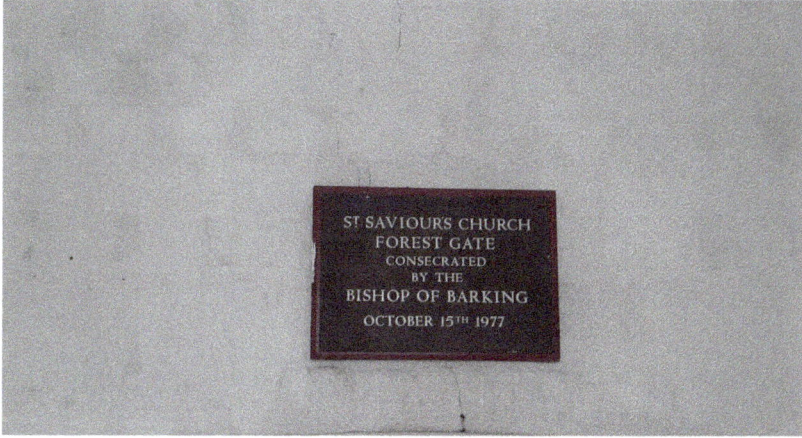

Plaque commemorating consecration of 'new' St Saviour's

Inside St Saviour's

The organ loft in St Saviour's

Holy Trinity banner

Resurrection banner

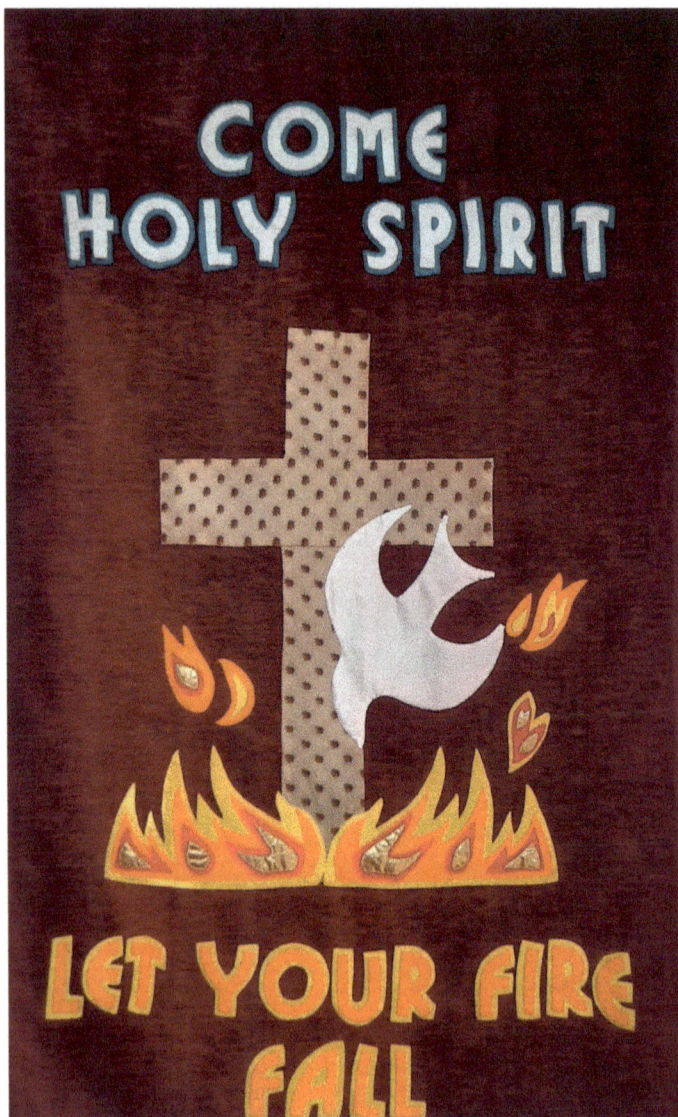

Come Holy Spirit banner

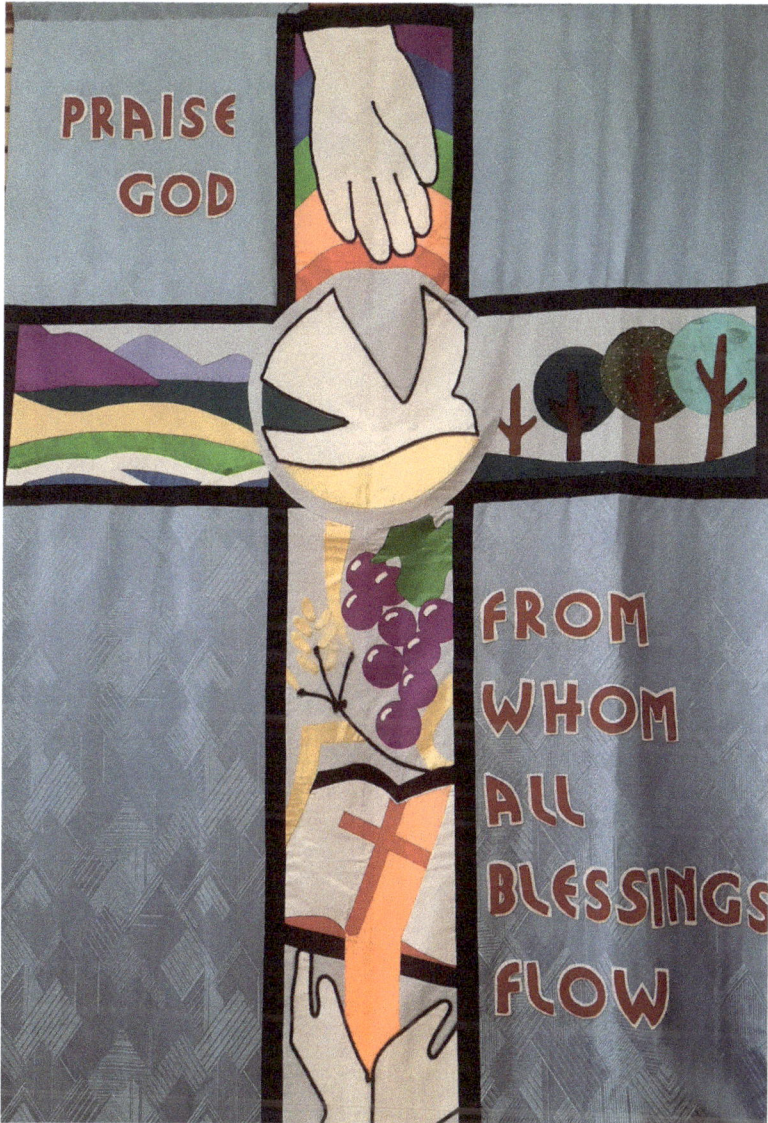

Praise God from Whom All Blessings Flow banner

Church outing in the 1970's possibly Maldon

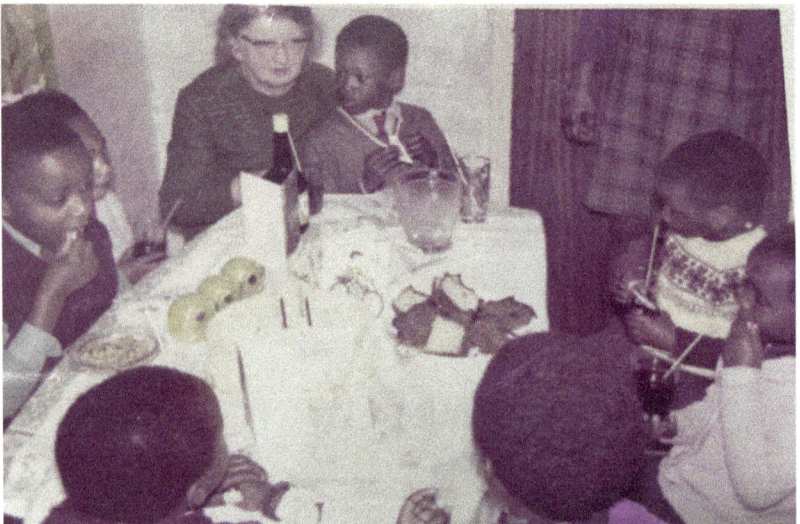

The increasing diversity of the community.
A young Ambrose celebrates his birthday with
members of the Armstrong and Graham families.

A Church trip to Jerusalem, the coast at Caesarea

Parish Weekend at Wetheringsett Manor 1990

16 September 2017

St Saviours Church
Forest Gate
40th Ruby Anniversary
Dinner & Dance

6:00 pm

St Saviours Church Forest Gate
Macdonald Road, Forest Gate, London E7 0HE
Tickets £15 Adult £10 Child

Church celebrated 40 years in its current building in 2017

Evangelism and Outreach

In the Jubilee booklet, under the heading 'A Missionary Church', the author writes, 'the Church people of St Saviour have always been noted for their Missionary zeal' (Woods 1934, p.34). Of the many societies and missionary agencies in existence or that emerged during the 19th century, it was the Church Missionary Society (CMS), founded in 1799, that was the principal society supported by and supporting work in the parish. The first vicar, Henderson Burnside, had come to the parish almost direct from CMS work in Japan. He had been one of the first Anglican missionaries in Japan and continued at St Saviour's to be very supportive of foreign missions. Closer to home we read that St Saviour's at that time also used an area under the railway, 365 Railway Arches, which for some time acted as a church hall for its mission work.

Evangelism and mission work is of course a continued theme. In 1987 Rev. John Williams says at the AGM of 13th April, 'worship is important, but evangelism is equally so for that is why we are here, but the ever-present temptation is to stay in the shallow and play it safe'. The great need is 'to launch out into the deep' to obtain 'a great catch'. Formation of an Evangelistic Committee is referred to at various times over the decades. Early on in Rev. Williams' incumbency, at the meeting of 16th March 1967 evangelistic plans for the year were discussed with various suggestions – open air meetings, films, services, 'Harvester' type groups. This was then 'left to the Evangelistic Committee to thrash out'!

It is clear in the parish records that the consecration of the new St Saviour's, in October 1977, was seen as an opportunity to plan and carry out some outreach activities. At the AGM of April 1977, some months after the building work commenced to create the new St Saviour's, the vicar makes the point that; 'our main concern is the spiritual building up and reaching out and praying'. The 'Parish Autumn Outreach' programme in 1977 included the delivery of cards to doors in the parish inviting people to come and see the new Church during the week of August 22nd to 25th. During September there was a visitation of lay persons to inform parishioners of the existence of the Church, its purpose and functions. In the event only a small part of the parish received publicity directly but the effort resulted in 40 people coming to see the Church and 15 of these then attended services. The AGM minutes of 1978 comment on 'an encouraging autumn outreach … Spiritual growth had been evident as well as the building of brick and mortar. Quite a number of new people are coming into the fellowship and benefits are still being reaped by the parish visitation'.

Open-Air Meetings and Services

References to open-air meetings appear in the minutes of PCC meetings over a number of decades. On 19th May 1959, the vicar suggests holding a series of open-air meetings in the parish during the summer perhaps twice a month. Open-air witness is a point of discussion at the meeting of 28th April 1962. On 21st January 1963 there is a suggestion that, for the open-air work in June, an amplifier be bought rather than borrowed. In September we learn that the amplifier usually borrowed has now been given to the Church. At the meeting of 15th March 1966, following a report from the Evangelistic Committee, it was agreed to start open-air meetings on Sunday evenings at the beginning of June. And each time a different road would be visited and cards, notifying occupants of the meetings, would be delivered to the houses of the relevant street during the preceding week. The commitment to using these meetings to try and encourage newcomers to the Church and provide a good experience for those gathered is evident. It is noted at the meeting for 26th May 1966 that a second hand portable organ has been purchased for £20 for open air meetings.

Church member Jean Murphy remembers the open-air meetings in the Church grounds and there is reference to these occurring in September 1990 after the evening service. She also recalls gathering on the corner of Forest Lane and Woodgrange Road after evening service. Minutes in October 1990 report that open-air meetings have been well supported by the congregation and again in January 1991 when, surprisingly, three open-air services had been held in December 1990. In late 1991 joint open-air meetings are being planned with the church then using nearby Bignold Hall. Over these decades though there is no clear statement as to whether these meetings and services brought longer-term newcomers to services at St Saviour's, and Jean's memory is that such meetings did not bring any newcomers. But at least they served to highlight the existence of an active church. In addition to open-air services and prayer meetings in specific roads, parish marches were instituted in order to raise the profile of the Church. These replaced the morning service once a year and the congregation would march round the whole parish and stop at many points to pray for the people in the street concerned.

The current vicar, the Reverend Cornelius Henry, undertakes regular prayer walks around the parish which now includes the parish of the former St James Church. Leaflets are also regularly distributed to inform the community of St Saviour's services and food bank. This is done mostly at Easter and Christmas, but also prayer leaflets delivered throughout the year inform the different roads in the parish that they are being prayed for and encourage residents to send in their prayer requests and join in services.

Wanstead Flats

Most of these open-air meetings then seemed to occur at the Church or on the streets of the parish. We know that very much earlier on in the twentieth century nearby Wanstead Flats was used as a gathering point for religious purposes by different churches and denominations (Wanstead Flats Working Group 2019). The space available was an obvious advantage but permission had to be sought as, following the 1878 Epping Forest Act, Wanstead Flats were managed by the City of London. An Epping Forest Committee was set up to oversee activities on Forest Lands (Wanstead Flats Working Group 2019). During the First World War an Intercession Service was held on Wanstead Flats at which over 2,000 people gathered. In St Saviour's parish magazine the vicar's letter of 24th June 1916 records this gathering on a wet afternoon, 'one cannot help feeling it to be the best possible sign of both the people's need and the way in which the minds of men are moving'. The letter announces a further service to be held at the bandstand on Wanstead Flats on 9th July at 3.15pm prompt, at which the Bishop of Chelmsford would be speaking.

Decades on and during the 1990s Decade of Evangelism, the Bishop of Barking had ambitious plans for a massive Pentecost 95 celebration on Wanstead Flats. Minutes of the DCC meeting of 6th June 1994 record that it is to be 'a celebration of London Life for all Faiths or none', and ideally the culmination of a week of mission by local churches. The date chosen was Saturday 3rd June 1995 and it was hoped to attract 5,000 for a picnic and worship. But, sadly, the DCC minutes of 12th June 1995 record that the event was rained off.

In recent years, St Saviours and other local churches have come together on two occasions on Sunday afternoons in celebration of Pentecost, holding family days on Wanstead Flats which combine a picnic and activities with opportunities to pray and worship together, and to find out more about the churches. And on these occasions the weather has proved much more favourable! The Flats are also normally the starting point for the Good Friday Walk of Witness through Forest Gate. Local churches come together to make this journey in silence stopping off at churches along the way for prayer and a song. It is an event that marks the sense of solidarity between the churches in the area. We know that this procession with other churches goes back some way. For example, a PCC meeting for 25th November 1965 records plans for Easter services the following year which includes a united service at Emmanuel preceded by a procession of witness.

Decade of Evangelism

The last decade of the 20th century saw an evangelistic drive which encompassed most Christian denominations including the Roman Catholic Church and the Lutheran Church. There was some agreement that national initiatives should be focussed around three years specifically 1994, 1997 and 2000. Each Diocese would also respond with its own initiatives (Francis and Roberts 2009).

Some of the initiatives planned for the1990s referred to in parish meeting minutes are:

4th June 1990: there is mention of Newham People's Festival 1st July and a carnival procession to start at Wanstead Flats finishing at Central Park. It was hoped to have a Christian float.

1st February 1993: refers to an Evangelistic Weekend on the 1st and 2nd May. The May weekend was combined with a barbecue which worked well in attracting people and on the Sunday there was a 'Praise March'.

6th December 1993: refers to 'On Fire' evangelistic training events at the Church and also a National March for Jesus.

Throughout 1994: there were prayers for revival on the first Friday of every quarter. Jean Murphy remembers that this was held in the Rectory.

31st January 1994: refers to four Missionary Sundays with a guest speaker and bread and cheese lunch.

4th March 1994: an 'On Fire' month of mission was planned to begin on 21st May and it was aimed to have morning Communion outside the Church on 22nd May at which the congregation would welcome onlookers in. A parish day out was also planned as a follow-up to 'On Fire'.

12th June 1994: a march around the parish was planned with prayers to be said for each street visited.

3rd June 1995: There has already been mention of the Bishop of Barking's plan for a Pentecost picnic and worship on Wanstead Flats in summer 1995 which unfortunately was rained off.

At the DCC meeting of 10th May 1999 as the Church approaches the new millennium the Five Marks of Mission are reiterated: 'To proclaim the good news of the Kingdom; to teach and baptise and nurture new believers; to respond to human need by loving service; to seek to transform the unjust structures of society; to strive to safeguard the integrity of creation and sustain and renew the life of the earth'. A Global March for Jesus was planned for Whitsun 2000.

Ann Turner was reminded, having found some of the posters that were used at the time, that the Church held a millennium exhibition in 2000 telling the story of Jesus as part of a general Church of England celebration. With no proper display area, Church members constructed a display unit using MDF.

Evangelical Work in the Asian Community

St Saviour's parish records tell us something of the evangelical work within the Asian community at this time which was being led by the Finnish Evangelical Lutheran Mission (FELM), formerly the Finnish Missionary Society. During the 1970s a number of teams from the FELM came to St Saviour's. Firm friendships were made between members of the congregation and the Finns who came that continued long after they had returned to Finland.

In particular Reino Servio from the FELM was seconded to the staff of St Saviour's for a period of eight years. This had been arranged from Finland through the Bible Churchmen's Missionary Society (B.C.M.S.) here. The FELM felt called to take the Gospel to members of the Asian community and saw an opportunity to work in Newham because of the growing Asian population. St Saviour's was approached because of its reputation as an evangelical church. Reino reported to the Church's AGM on his work and eventually published a booklet on the Asian community in Newham. In 1979 he reported that he had visited 160 Asian families in the area, many of them in their own homes. By 1982 the increasing impact of racial tensions was evident and racial troubles in October 1981 were referred to specifically. Reino reported that although he was still being welcomed, some of the Asian families he visited did not want to hear about the Christian faith. Very tellingly, he said, 'The Asian community are very worried'. DCC minutes of March 1991 refer to Pippa of the FELM and her intention to hold a Bible Study group for Sikh girls one evening a week at St Saviour's.

Päivi Takala was also active in this outreach work to the Asian community and, as we have heard, she was instrumental in setting up the Parent/Carer and Toddler Group at the Church. But in 1993 she returned to Finland when the FELM had to withdraw all its workers abroad due to a financial recession in the country. However she married Church member Stephen Pratt in 1994 and returned to live temporarily in Forest Gate in 1995, in one of the flats on the site of the old St Saviour's.

National Missions over the Decades

Billy Graham Crusades: Billy Graham's first crusade in England was in 1954. Videos on YouTube of Pathe News are evidence of the incredible enthusiasm for the American evangelist. The year 1954 was known as the Greater London Crusade during which every night thousands filled the Harringey Arena in North London to hear Graham speak. A coach load from St Saviour's went to the last meeting of the 12 week crusade at Wembley Stadium in 1954 when 10,000 converts came forward to commit their life to Christ. At a meeting of 5th May 1961 plans were being made for relays in a marquee in Stratford of the Billy Graham meeting in Manchester in June.

Graham's last mission in England, known as Mission England, was in 1989. One of the venues chosen was at West Ham United football ground then in Upton Park. Graham appeared there on

14th, 15th and 16th June. St Saviour's was one of 900 churches to have registered their support for the Mission and each church was asked to nominate four people for various tasks. This was discussed at a DCC meeting in January 1989 when four were appointed as follows: Ray Vincent for men's work; Ruth Ruwana for women's work; Ambrose Gordon for youth work and Stella Olukanmi as co-ordinator – 'in preparation for the coming mission Christian life and witness classes will be held at Highway Hall during Lent'. Ray remembers that members of the Church helped out with stewarding at the crusade meetings. Jean Murphy recalls that five members of St Saviour's joined the crusade choir which was made up of various churches throughout the borough. She also remembers the amazing atmosphere in London during the crusade when underground trains were regularly crowded with hymn singing passengers on their way to the rally. In October 1989, the vicar reported that as a direct result of Mission 89 a discovery group had met for six weeks. Six adults were worshipping regularly who had not been worshipping before. Other members of the congregation had recommitted their lives.

Other Missionary Events include:

Radio Mission: Radio Mission services were broadcast by the BBC in 1954 and in July 1954 copies of Radio Mission letters were to be delivered to each house in the parish if possible, along with a personal invitation to come to the Church. St Saviour's invited the local Methodist church to join them in the week's mission. At a meeting of 13th December 1954 the comment is made that Radio Mission had proved to be a time for refreshing for members of the church but was 'not reaching outsiders or backsliders'!

Luis Palau Mission to London: In May 1984 an Argentinian evangelist, Luis Palau, conducted a mission to London which took place at Queens Park Rangers football ground for six weeks. A coach load from St Saviour's attended on one of the days. As well as this mission there was a mission to Newham led by Doug Barnett, born in Poplar.

Mustard Seed 1987: The Church was asked to join in sending teams to inner city areas for outreach as part of Mustard Seed 1987. Mustard Seed was committed to working in inner city areas to enable churches and encourage them to evangelise in their parishes. The Church acted as host to a visiting team of ten, six of whom stayed in the church hall where they could use the kitchen to prepare breakfast and there was a rota for people offering evening meals. The team was around for 14 days starting with an induction weekend and a fish and chip supper to provide an opportunity for everyone to meet up.

New Wine: A 'missional agency' founded in 1989 with a vision 'to see local churches renewed, strengthened, connected, empowered and alive with the fullness and presence of God', New Wine offered local and national events, initially held in the West Country. Marie Duggan, as she was then, remembers that Rev. John Williams, for many years, took a group from the Church to New Wine gatherings. The younger people, including Marie, would also work as part of the teams at New Wine. It was a time for her of 'a lot of blessings', and although she now attends another church her time at St Saviour's was an 'amazing' part of her life. Andy Spraggs, who first visited New Wine in 2005, had, for a time, attended St Barnabas Church, Finchley, where the vicar, Rev. John Cole, later became director of New Wine.

Soul Survivor : Soul Survivor grew from New Wine. Founded in 1993 by Mike Pilavachi it started as Soul Survivor Watford and is now a global Christian movement which has overseen many summer festivals for young people. 2019 marked the last year of festivals but Soul Survivor runs other events during the year through its church in Watford and resources on its website. Leah Gordon remembers the impact attending Soul Survivor had on her and hearing speakers such as Mike Pilavachi and Andy Croft: 'The first time I went I must admit the spiritual connection that I had with God was amazing and from that point I realised that God had come into my life in ways I hadn't realised.' The last night of the festivals always involved a fancy dress theme.

Recent Mission Work

Through Faith Missions (TFM) 2019: This took place in Stratford and Forest Gate from 3rd to 12th May 2019. It encompassed four churches: St Saviour's, St Paul's, St Matthews, St John's. TFM sends trained people to work with churches and aim to train people in basic evangelism. A training session was held at St Saviour's on 4th May. Activities included prayer walks and house-to-house visits whereby those participating in the Mission knocked on doors to talk to people about faith. A very well-attended family fun day was held on the bank holiday Monday in the children's play area in Magpie Close. Along with activities, games and food, there was a prayer ministry.

Charity Mission

As with all churches there is a long history of supporting charitable causes and activities. In recent years 12 Christian based charities, one for each month, have been highlighted specifically for donations of at least £100 and the charity is prayed for throughout the month. The list is reviewed periodically by a committee of the PCC and a service each year is dedicated to the charities.

One of the major activities that the whole Church became involved in starting in the 1990s is Operation Christmas Child. This is organised by the charity Samaritan's Purse, with the aim of sharing God's love in a tangible way to children in need around the world, and to share the Good News of Christmas.

The idea to become involved came from Iris Head and her daughter, and was carried on by Angela Prince. Initially members filled their boxes and brought them to Church. Over the years it has developed into a much larger scale operation requiring considerable organisation which for some years was overseen by Ray Vincent and Angela. Now members of the congregation bring items to go in the boxes such as colouring books, pencils and toys, soap, flannels and toothbrushes. Other members engage in knitting woolly hats and other items such as scarves and pencil cases. Shoe boxes also need to be collected and covered with appropriate paper and in recent years the covering has been done almost single-handedly by one Church member, Georgina Leadeham. The last stage is when Church members come together, usually mid-November, to fill the boxes and also contribute to distribution costs. In this way, the Church has recently been able to send over 100 filled boxes a year to Operation Christmas Child.

Ecumenical and Shared Activities

St Saviours Church was a member of the Forest Gate Council of Christian Churches (FGCCC) which included Anglican, Baptist, Methodist and Roman Catholic Churches. Representatives met together on a regular basis and various united events were held during Lent and Easter, and Jean Murphy recalls that every year there was also a United Hymn Festival. DCC minutes of 22nd January 1990 refer to an ecumenical garden party to be held at St Angela's Convent on 5th July.

According to Wilson (1995) the Council was most active in the 1960s, though at the PCC meeting in January 1960, a point is made that there is a need to look at what FGCCC should be doing to be effective, which suggests some uncertainty as to whether it was fulfilling its purpose. In April 1962 the vicar reads out plans for the united visitation of part of the parish under the sponsorship of the FGCCC which is to take place at the end of May. Interestingly at the DCC meeting in October 1989 there is discussion around whether the FGCC should be more involved in social action and making a bigger impact in community, though no firm conclusion is reached. In 1990 the Council became known as Churches Together in Forest Gate. By 1994 it had become a more informal group. By March 1997 it had been disbanded.

Much more recently, for a few years during Rev. Henry's incumbency, monthly Sunday evening services were held on a rota basis across a number of churches – All Saints Manor Park, St Emmanuel's, St Mark's, St Saviour's, Woodgrange Baptist Church and the Woodgate Community. The musical abilities of members of the latter, as well as those of St Mark's, greatly added to the experience and included the (unrehearsed) singing of parts of Handel's Messiah at Easter and Christmas. The churches usually come together for carol singing in Forest Gate market area every Christmas. Sadly for our community, the Woodgate Community moved to a larger property in South London.

In the 1960s some controversy over plans for activities involving non-conformist ministers in an Easter service is recorded. At the meeting of 6th February 1964, the vicar sounded out the PCC on the question of holding a united Communion service in St Saviours for members of the FGCCC in which ministers of the free churches would take part. All the non-conformist ministers accepted the invitation to join the service but permission was not forthcoming from the Bishop, though he stated his sympathy for the project. A copy of a letter was filed with the PCC minutes of 27th April 1964 recording the concern over this decision. It requested that, whatever the differences, the Church of England did not go back on its hospitality to free churchmen: 'we deprecate deeply this retrograde step which has been interpreted by the press as 'the Church of England shutting the door on free churchmen'. A further attempt to hold a united Communion service on Maundy Thursday was made in 1966 but the Bishop again 'did not give permission for the chalice to be administered by a non-conformist'.

Members of the different churches also come together at Easter and Christmas time to work with the organisation Faith in Schools hosting and supporting interactive sessions for local school children that enable them to participate in and learn about the Easter and Christmas stories.

People

The reports produced for the annual meetings of the parish always demonstrate the importance of the Church membership in supporting the vicar in the running of the Church and its activities. In 2022, 83 members are listed on the electoral roll though that does not necessarily include all who attend. Much of the work within a church therefore is undertaken by members who contribute their talents, time and energies to unpaid roles at many different levels whether it be cleaning, serving coffee, welcoming, reading, leading intercessions, membership of the Parochial Church Council (PCC) – the list can be very long! All of these are regarded as ministries. Many names are referred to throughout this publication but there is not space here to name or to detail the immense commitment of so many who have willingly served the Church both in paid and unpaid roles. So we have selected a few names from the past that are still very meaningful to current members, as well as including thoughts from those now undertaking the role of church warden.

Vicars since 1880

Rev. H. Burnside 1880-1903; Rev. A.N. Rae 1903-1916; Rev. C. Spencer 1916-1919; Rev. C.J.A. Burden 1920-1931; Rev. W.H. Rowdon 1931-1934; Rev. R. Williams 1934-1941; Rev. W.B. Thomas 1942-1946; Rev. B.C. Aldis 1946-1951; Rev. H.T. Blake 1952-1957; Rev. C.H. Hampton 1957-1964; Rev. Canon John Williams 1965-2012; Rev. Cornelius A. Henry 2013-.

The content of the Jubilee booklet of 1934 is arranged in chapters for each incumbency from Rev. Burnside to Rev. Rowdon accompanied by a photograph of each vicar. The vicar at time of

publication, who also wrote the introduction, was the Rev. Ralph
Williams (Woods 1934).

Reverend Canon John Williams

John Williams was the well-loved vicar of St Saviour's for much of
the period we are focussing on. He took up his incumbency in
1965, following the Rev. C H Hampton, and he retired in 2012.
He moved away to Wiltshire and then to be with family in Bristol.
Very sadly he died quite suddenly in April 2020 during the
lockdown period in the Covid-19 pandemic. Although his health
in retirement was not good, to the very end John had a wonderful
memory and recall of detail and was always able to answer
questions asked of him about the past which has been of great
value to this history. We were hoping to capture much more
information and detail from him for this history but unfortunately
that was not to be.

When the Rev. Hampton had announced that he was leaving to
move to a small country parish near Dorchester, he had said that
he 'felt that a younger man with a lot of vim is needed in the
parish'. In an article from the *Newham Recorder* written at the
time of his retirement John Williams said, 'when I first came I had
no experience of the area, but it was a good challenge. I thought
I'll try to fit in but if I don't I'll just move on,' (Kvist 2012).

But John fitted in well. He brought fresh energy and enthusiasm
and made a considerable impact on the spiritual and social life of
the Church. His forward thinking led to growth in the membership
of the Church. Jean Murphy whose Church membership covered
much of the period of John's ministry, says that John was very
interested in the charismatic movement which was coming to the
fore nationally during his ministry, and St Saviour's members used
to go regularly to charismatic meetings in London with John and
lady worker, Betty Osborne. They would go to Fountain Trust
meetings which were normally held at the Methodist Central Hall,
Westminster, during the 1970s. Fountain Trust was an ecumenical

organisation promoting the charismatic renewal. Jean writes of John, 'his life-long passion was for revival to come to the Church. He certainly brought revival to St Saviour's through his ministry and he stretched the mind of the congregation with his enthusiasm in believing that all things were possible through the work of the Holy Spirit'.

John himself especially loved the fact that increasingly during his ministry the local area became more multi-cultural and that this was reflected in the make-up of the Church. The late Lyris Williams, a long-time member of the Church who came to England from Barbados, recalled how good a leader John Williams was and how he treated everyone the same. She remarked, 'When I was in hospital for six weeks he came to see me every day phoning the nurses first to find out if there was anything I needed, because I had no family here. He was just like a brother to me.'

In the parish magazine, for October 1965, the only one that still exists from John's ministry, and a few months after his ministry began, John's sense of humour definitely comes through. This is how he starts the magazine, '1970 and All That: Everyone is thinking about 1970. The government is, the trade unions are, the employers are, and so are members of St Saviour's Council ... '.

Members of the Church recall his wit and use of opportunities for jokes, often the kind of jokes that were simultaneously enjoyed and groaned at!

During this time John was also Senior Canon at Chelmsford Cathedral and involved in delivering services there.

Past Church Wardens

The role of the wardens is very important in the church as the wardens have a duty to represent the laity and cooperate with and support the incumbent and to help ensure the smooth running of the church and maintenance of the building. The wardens are also members of the PCC which is the main decision making body of a parish. The commitment and workload of wardens is certainly clear from the archives and here we include two from past decades who are remembered by Church members and who between them gave almost 70 years of service as wardens.

H W Barnard: Throughout much of the earlier decades we are focussing on from the 1940s through to the 1960s Harold Barnard served the Church in various roles including treasurer, secretary and church warden. He is invariably referred to as HW Barnard in records. The administrative archives on the maintenance of the Church building and many other aspects, pay tribute to his role as secretary in the considerable amount of correspondence that bears his name. It is also evident in the minutes of meetings in the early sixties how much he was offering to undertake. He, his wife and his sister Eileen were all prominent members of the Church and all contributed much to the running of the Church, only a small amount of which is likely recorded in minutes. In a remaining copy of the Church Magazine for October 1961 HW Barnard is described as lay reader and church warden. In May 1966 he takes on the position of secretary for the annual bazaar quite possibly because there was no-one else forthcoming. In November 1967, once it is known that the proposed amalgamation of St James' and St Saviour's was not going through, it is HW Barnard who proposes the setting up of a special committee to consider the whole question of the old St Saviour's church building and, in particular, suggests that a long term view be taken. By the 1970s Jean Murphy recalls that Mr and Mrs Barnard had moved from Forest Gate, though Eileen Barnard remained local and became a good friend of Jean's. At the PCC meeting in June 1977, when plans were being made for the consecration of the new St Saviour's, Mr and Mrs Barnard are specifically mentioned as guests to be invited, which seems an acknowledgement of their considerable contribution.

Ken Jupp who died in 2005 was church warden for over 40 years. He is remembered by Church members who knew him as being particularly dedicated and conscientious, and he spent much time at the Church ensuring that all sorts of tasks were done to aid its smooth running. Pauline Haywood describes him as 'a very faithful servant' who never knew the meaning of delegation. And in the same vein Jean Murphy writes, 'he could always be relied upon to carry out faithfully the duties of churchwarden'. But taking his role so seriously he could also be very strict at times and Pauline's children remember this. For example her eldest son remembers Ken telling him off for wearing his cap in church. And Jean describes him as 'formidable' on occasions, especially at PCC meetings. But both Pauline and Jean recall how caring Ken could also be. He was very supportive of Pauline as an assistant church warden and would transport her and look after her at the annual swearing in service for wardens. Equally he was very ready to give much needed support to anyone going through a difficult time, and Jean can testify to this personally. Ken died very suddenly while he was still warden and a plaque in the Church acknowledges his considerable service.

Present Wardens record some of their thoughts on how they came to take up this role

Pauline Haywood: While Ken Jupp was church warden, at the AGM of April 1999 Pauline and Roy Graham were elected as deputy wardens. Pauline had acted as a sidesperson before being elected first as a deputy warden and recalls:

> Ken supported me for many years, until his sudden death. I was supported by the congregation to apply for the warden's role. I applied and to my amazement I got the job. I absolutely enjoyed being the warden, how wonderful to be doing the Lord's work, so many people come to me for support and advice, and also if things are not going well. St Saviour's has helped me to grow, giving me confidence in speaking, praying, listening, and giving me some great colleagues and friends. The Lord has held my hands, heart and every step, leading me to where he wanted me.

Although Pauline has now stepped down from her role as warden, her past and ongoing contribution is honoured by the special title of Church Warden Emeritus.

Noel Morris, church warden at time of writing recalls:

I started to attend St Saviours in 2005 and was confirmed in 2007. As I attended I began to think that there must be something I can do within the Church and I became a sidesperson for some time. But then I said to myself there must be something more I can do. When the post of assistant warden came up I was approached by several members of the Church to apply for it which I did, and, to my amazement, I got the job. I had the pleasure of working with the then church wardens, Pauline Haywood and Roy Graham. They were amazing to work with and very supportive. They taught me a lot and as a result I grew in confidence. When Roy sadly passed away I took on the role of church warden.

Being a church warden is very challenging but it can be exciting as well. The role involves a lot. It is part of my role to make sure the building is secure and records up to date. I aim to assist the vicar as much as possible and try to ensure that the building is safe and comfortable for all those attending on Sundays. I regularly check round the building, inside and out, to see if everything is okay and do whatever I can, and make sure any problems are highlighted to the PCC. Talking to members of the congregation as much as possible is an important part of my role. Equally, confidence gained through taking on this role has helped and encouraged me in my interactions with the many people I meet as part of being a church warden, as well as enriching my spiritual life.

I give God thanks and praise for without him I don't think I would be able to cope. And I thank my warden and deputy warden colleagues – Pauline, Doreen, David and Grace, for all their help and pray that the Lord will continue to bless them to carry on the good work they are doing for the Church.

Mention must also be made of Noel's wife, Maxine, who undertakes a considerable amount of background support for many of the Church's activities.

Grace Ani:

I joined the Church in 1987 and found it to be a family friendly church. Having read about the role of warden I considered applying in the 1990s but felt I already had too many responsibilities, including my professional career. I became involved in various church activities and I was elected a member of the PCC during the following decade. As years went by I was increasingly conscious of the importance and responsibility of the warden's role, which if done conscientiously will augment the effort of the clergy to encourage the congregation, and will then strengthen the body of Christ, the church. So, encouraged by Church members I was pleased to apply in 2019 and was voted in. As the most recently elected warden I'm still learning and gaining experience. As wardens we are actively supporting and counselling church members in line with church teachings. It is an exciting as well as a challenging role but being a committed Christian and a prayer warrior, it is an amazing service to God.

Doreen Alexander, former deputy warden:

I joined St Saviour's in 1994 when I took my daughter to be christened, a year later I was confirmed. A few months after that I was elected as a member of the PCC and deputy churchwarden, I became PCC secretary, a job which I did for 24 years until I stepped down September 2021. Much of this period of time was while John Williams was minister. We are a very close knit church we are always there to help each other and to support anyone in need as the Bible teaches us.

Doreen remains very active. She continues as a safeguarding officer and, as part of a rota of members, regularly leads the service, undertakes readings and intercessions as well as being a member of the prayer team. Doreen makes the point that a lot of the work that goes on behind the scenes is done by volunteers. As an example, when John Williams retired after 47 years as vicar, a team of volunteers was responsible for running the church until the Rev. Cornelius Henry was appointed.

David Beaumont, deputy church warden. Appointment to this role and that of synod rep. has helped David to feel much more involved in church life, engaged and motivated.

Additional Staffing

We have snippets of information about paid staff over the years who helped with the running of the Church and its activities. In the 1950s there are references to Sister Howell a paid lady worker connected with the Church Army. She helped with the running of some of the groups such as Brownies, and with the Sunday school work. Sister Howell had to resign in early 1957 because of family illness. A replacement was needed but it proved quite difficult to find one. In January 1958 we read that there is an opportunity to appoint a curate at a salary of £375 a year and one is appointed but never took up the position because of difficulties finding appropriate accommodation. In 1959 at least one student from the London Bible College (now the London School of Theology) was assisting.

In July 1960 the Reverend Hampton, needing a paid worker's help, approached the London City Missionary. The Mission employed full-time workers often deliberately selected from the working classes and not ordained in any way, who visited people regularly and befriended them, helping them practically as well as spiritually (London City Mission n.d.). According to minutes from 27th January 1961 the London City Missionary bought a house, no 22 Hampton Road, Forest Gate, and a Mr S Ritchie started work in the parish. He seems to have participated in some of the open-air work and also did work with young people. He then moved to north London. In a parish magazine that still exists from July 1961, Mr Ritchie is listed as missioner.

Betty Osborne. Long-time Church members remember with fondness lady worker, Betty Osborne. While working as a district nurse she had been a member of the Church and helped with Sunday school. The PCC minutes of 6th August 1965 record that

Betty Osborne is to start as lady worker on September 19th. This is confirmed in one of the few remaining parish magazines, October 1965, which refers to the newly appointed lady worker Miss Osborne, and hope is expressed that she will be welcomed into homes and prayed for regularly. At this point she is working for a quarter of her time for the Ladies' Home Mission Union (LHMU) and the remainder with St Saviour's. She is a popular choice with both members and funding bodies. Her starting salary is £800 per annum and correspondence in the archives reflects the concern, as ever, about raising sufficient funds. The funding came from a combination of the LHMU, the London-over-the-Border Church Fund ((LOB) and the Church Pastoral Aid Society (CPAS). The PCC minutes of the 24th April 1967 record that there is now the possibility of Betty Osborne working full time as a lady worker in the parish. An approach is then made to the Diocese for funding. The 21st November 1967 minutes confirm a diocesan contribution to the salary. We also learn that a trainee lady worker from St Michael's House Oxford, Miss Costan, is to work in the parish for ten weeks from January 1968.

Betty Osborne was to remain as a lady worker at St Saviour's until well into the 1980s. She was a major influence in the life of the Church. As well as helping with the organisation of the house parties she also led a Bible Study group, regular prayer meetings, arranged the flowers each week and assisted John at the Sunday services. She took a part in leading the choir, rehearsing the hymns with the choir each week and recruiting members. Betty was instrumental in starting Open House, described earlier. She also organised Church outings. The parish records for the 1960s and 1970s show the impact that an extra person with passion had on initiatives and driving things forward, and involving people. Jean Murphy, who became a close friend of Betty's, describes her as a, 'Lynchpin in the life of St Saviour's Church,' and comments that, 'Her Christian faith shone through everything she did for our Lord.' One thing that pleased Betty in her visits to West Indian families in the parish was how well she became accepted by them, because they were happy to invite her into their kitchens.

In 1986, with Betty Osborne's retirement on the horizon, there is more emphasis on lay ministry in discussions: 'DCC members should regard themselves as spiritual leaders and be prepared to share lay leadership'. This obviously has some effect as at the AGM in April 1989 when the vicar remarks that the past year had been one of the most encouraging years since he started at St Saviour's, one of the reasons is 'greater lay participation in worship and services'.

And in 2022 ...

At time of writing in 2022 the Church is very fortunate to have the Rev. Janetta Brathwaite as curate at St Saviour's. She joined the Church in 2020 as a self-supporting minister for a three-year training period and was ordained in September in 2020. In addition, as from January 2022 Katherine Bennett joined the Church as ordinand, in training to be ordained as a minister. Along with much-loved and respected vicar, Rev. Cornelius Henry, the Church is greatly enriched by all this participation, including that of a vibrant membership.

Sunday Services

Apart from the early 20th century parish magazines, there are only two that remain up until very recent times and these are from the 1960s. The services listed in the October 1965 issue are: Holy Communion (first and third Sundays at 8am ; second and fifth Sundays at 6.30pm.; fourth Sunday at 11am); Divine Services at 11am and 6.30pm. At that time the evening services were better attended and the vicar, John Williams, commented on this, 'less than 30 people came to the Sunday sermon while 40-45 people would attend the evening service' (Kvist 2012).

As a result the PCC meeting of September 1972 records the start of communion every Sunday at the 6.30 pm service, and once a month there was communion after the morning service. The AGM minutes of 1972 refer to 'Sunday Night Extra' held after the evening service. Jean Murphy remembers attending these when services were held in the church hall as the old St Saviour's became less and less usable. She describes the Sunday Night Extra as 'a time for fellowship, choruses and discussion'.

There seems to be then something of a shift to popularity of the morning service and at some point it had become a 10.30am start. In February 1982 morning Communion service is reported as being a great success. And by the 1990s there is an established pattern of communion on the second and fourth Sundays of the month, a pattern that continued until disrupted by the effects of the Covid-19 pandemic. Most of the Sunday services now are Communion Services. At the DCC meeting of 31 October 1988, under the heading 'future plans', the vicar suggested experimenting with serving tea and coffee after the morning service and this is now a well-established practice often with cakes included, especially if there are celebrations such as birthdays or baptisms.

In the DCC meeting for 28th September 1998 it is agreed that the evening service change to 5.30pm from 3rd January 1999 as an experiment for the period of a year. Jean recalls that the change was not very popular and possibly did not even last a year. This perhaps marked the end of regular evening services. Beryl Duggan remembers that the 'Come on and Celebrate' service, which has been mentioned previously, took the place of the regular evening service. Held monthly it was 'a contemporary worship service with an invitation for people from the community to attend'.

Something that almost certainly resonates with us now is a point made in the DCC meeting of 1st December 1997 on the need for a prompt start of the morning service at 10.30am rather than waiting for latecomers! This is reiterated in the AGM minutes in 2000 as 'services are getting later and later because of people's time-keeping'. The admonition continues, 'It should be possible for the congregation in most cases to get to church early in order to pray for the service, find the first hymn and read the Bible reading'. It is also said that the singing needs to improve!

The preface to this history refers to the impact of the Covid-19 pandemic on the church and ways of worship. The Church's annual report for 2020 records: March 23rd 2020, the government announced the lockdown of the country due to the Coronavirus pandemic. The Church of England ordered that all churches close their doors and broadcast services through media such as: Facebook, YouTube, Zoom or other online facilities. The last service at St Saviour's before lockdown was a very curtailed and scaled down Mother's Day service.

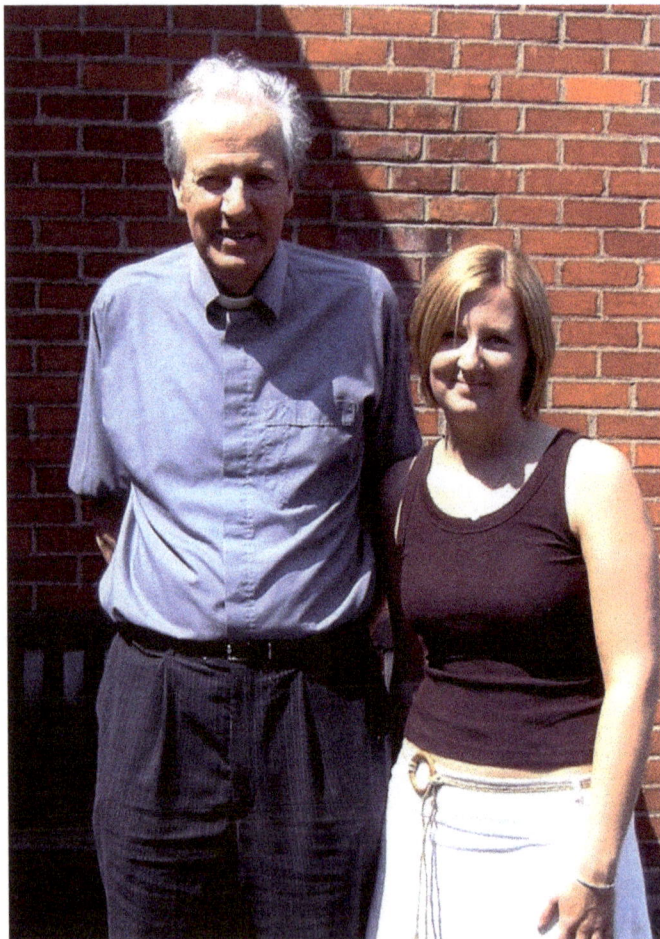

Rev. Canon John Williams with daughter Rachel

Rev. Canon John Williams in St Saviour's

Rev. Canon John Williams with a colleague

St Saviour's PCC members 2022

St Saviour's PCC members 2022

1907 Magazine

1965 Magazine

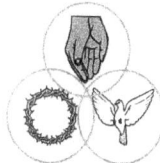

Parish magazines from different decades

Joint Working and Mergers

Proposals and outcomes

There is a definite sense of uncertainty in the records during meetings in early 1963 when there were discussions about church amalgamations in Forest Gate. St James' Church, like St Saviour's had originally been established in an iron building around 1870 before a parish was formed in 1881 and a permanent building consecrated in 1882, and was sited towards the Forest Lane end of St James Road. In 1961 the merger of St James' with Emmanuel was proposed. As a result of these proposals enquiries had been made about the future position of St Saviour's. The reply was that there were no further plans for any amalgamation in Forest Gate. However, on 4th March 1963 it is recorded that the PCC had been informed that 'we might still be brought into the discussion over the future of St James'. A year later the vicar was speaking about the revised plans regarding St James' parish 'which had been made without consultation with the clergy and people of the adjacent parishes'. The vicar 'spoke with some feeling on the whole question of reorganisation in Forest Gate'. In fact, St James' was demolished in 1964, after which its congregation met in the chapel of the Durning Hall community centre. In 1966 the parish of St James was united with that of St John's Stratford and became known as St James, Stratford. In 1968 a new St James' was built at the northern end of St James Road (BHO: British History Online 1973; Wikipedia 2022).

During 1964 however things remained uncertain. The Reverend Hampton was due to move to a smaller country parish. At the meeting of 1st September 1964 the church wardens presented various notices received from the Diocesan legal secretary regarding the impending vacancy and 'the Bishop's decision to apply Section 8 of the Pastoral Reorganisation Measure 1949 suspending the appointment of an incumbent until the question of the benefice being united or held in plurality with another, has been settled'. At the meeting on 12th October 1964 there is talk of an amalgamation of St Matthew's, West Ham, sited in Dyson Road, Stratford and St Saviour's, but concern was voiced because of the distance between the two churches. At the meeting of 9th April 1965 the decision that St Matthew's and St Saviour's are to retain separate identities is recorded.

By June 1965 there is discussion on the proposed merger of St James' and St Saviour's. This seems to be linked to the erection of a new St James' which would be a chapel-of-ease for the united parish and St Saviour's would be the parish church. At the meeting of 6th August 1965 it is recorded that St James' is not in favour of the merger on the grounds of churchmanship and the fact that they were beginning to be integrated into the life of St John's Stratford, a connection that was formalised in 1966. Despite this, by April 1967 there is a new proposal which, not surprisingly leads to a 'lengthy discussion'. It is proposed that the former parish of St James', now linked with St John's, dispose of sites and St Saviour's dispose of sites, with exception of the vicarage, and that a site in a central position in this area be obtained for a church and a hall. Not surprisingly the discussions in progress about the state of the old St Saviour's building have to be put aside. By the meeting of 21st November 1967 it is known that the proposed amalgamation of St James' and St Saviour's is not now going through and the minutes state, 'we are now in a position to reconsider what shall be done regarding repairs etc to the church'. A Building Committee is formed.

St Saviour's with St Matthew's

The uncertainty does not go away. At the meeting of 20th November 1968 it is recorded that the vicar spoke of 'the uncertainty of a Diocesan plan for this area', hence the delay in the Building Committee being able to submit its first report. Nearly two years on the meeting of 28th September 1970 records that there is a formal recommendation that St Matthew's, West Ham, be linked with St Saviour's. Another 18 months on at the meeting of 26th April 1972, two related items are recorded. One is that the legal process to unite the two parishes was being put into motion. The other is that John Betjeman has visited both St Saviour's and St Matthew's on behalf of the Council for the Care of Churches (now the Church Buildings Council). At the AGM of April 1973 the key preoccupations are the plans for the new St Saviour's and the union with St Matthew's. Minutes for the meeting on 19th August 1973 record that it was a stormy meeting over the draft scheme for uniting the two parishes. Work was also in progress on a constitution for the PCC of the new combined parish. On 2nd February 1975 an emergency meeting is called and confirms that the new St Saviour's will be the parish church in the new combined parish. The first of the combined PCC meetings for both churches is held on 14th April 1975 at St Matthew's. It is encouraging to read in the minutes of the AGM in April 1981 that there is a very positive Chair's report indicating a settled relationship with St Matthew's.

During this time a team ministry is established. A meeting in December 1975 records that the Bishop of Barking has said that a team ministry is to be set up. The meeting of 4th October 1976 confirms that the team ministry has come into effect from 1st September 1976. John Williams is designated Rector, and Alan Costerton at St Matthew's becomes Team Vicar. He is followed by the Reverend Robert (Bob) Love who commenced in October 1979.

St Saviour's with St James'

In October 2013 the parishes of St Saviour's and St Matthew's were separated. In September 2014 St James' Church Minister and Fellowship moved to join St Paul's Church Stratford. A Pastoral Order, effective 1st October 2014, transferred to St Saviour's part of the parish of St John and Christ Church, Stratford, with St James, including the former church of St James. St Saviour's was re-named St Saviour's with St James. The connection has enabled a greater role with nearby St James' School on Forest Lane and Tower Hamlets Road. The vicar is now chaplain to the school and takes assembly at the school every week in term time. He is also a foundation governor. Children from the school visit the Church by way of introduction to it and there have been other events such as a mock wedding, and a singing performance held in the Church. St Saviour's is also storing a World War commemoration plaque and a book of Remembrance from St James'. The church built at the northern end of St James's Road in 1968 has now been demolished. The site is reserved by the Diocese for the building of a new Rectory for the rector of St. Saviour. The current PCC has taken the view that they do not wish the Rectory to be relocated from Sidney Road to this site, so the plans are on hold for the time being.

Mission and Ministry Units

Since 2013 Mission and Ministry Units (MMU's) have been formed within the Diocese as part of the Transforming Presence strategy. An initiative of the previous Diocesan Bishop, Stephen Cottrell who is now the Archbishop of York, some MMUs are more established than others. The local one for St Saviour's also includes Emmanuel, St Mark's, All Saints Forest Gate, St Michael, and St Barnabas, Manor Park. The Units are intended to help to pool resources and support a sustainable ministry within each area.

Music at St Saviour's

The Organ

The story of St Saviour's organ which transferred from the old to the new St Saviour's is a remarkable one. The chief protagonist in this story, Anthony Dunhill, also known as Tony, has written a book about his extensive musical activities and St Saviour's organ (Dunhill 2016). From a very young age he was learning to play a range of instruments. He was very curious about the structures of different instruments and over the years undertook courses in piano-tuning and repair, and instrument-making at the London College of Furniture in Commercial Road. All of this prepared him well in his involvement with St Saviour's.

Tony had moved to Forest Gate in 1968 and joined St Saviour's just at the point when the then organist was moving away. He says, 'I became organist and choirmaster almost overnight!'(Dunhill 2016, p.27). War damage to the Church impacted on the organ and despite repairs increasingly there were problems due to leathers perishing over the years. In 1972, because of faulty electrical supply to the Church, the organ was no longer playable.

Not surprisingly it was not considered possible to transfer the organ to the new Church and purchase of an electronic organ was planned. Tony says very specifically that it was in May 1975 that the idea occurred to him that it might be possible to transfer the old organ without outside help. The old St Saviour's was about to be demolished so the PCC agreed that immediate steps be taken to dismantle and store the organ while the practicability of the proposal was examined. Time was short and Tony made use of contacts and friends who were organ experts and reached the conclusion that it was achievable, more cost effective than purchasing a new electronic alternative, and would provide a better quality and longer lasting instrument. Tony says, 'from the start the whole PCC and congregation were right behind the project. We felt that if God wanted us to go ahead and do this, then He would give us the skill, patience, time and money, and anything else we needed. We found out that this was just what happened, some of those things in quite remarkable ways' (Dunhill 2016, p.30). The dismantling work took 133 hours and involved the labelling of 1141 pipes. Tony even a created a special rack to store pipes under five feet to protect them. To store all of the parts took up a complete garage (the Rectory garage), a complete attic floor, half a cellar and parts of two lofts.

When it came to the reconstruction in the new St Saviour's a 10-foot high platform had been built above the entrance to house most of the organ except for the console and the seven largest pipes that had to rise from the floor beneath the platform. In June 1977, heavy component parts of the organ were moved onto the platform while builders were still working below. Members of the Church helped with moving, painting and cleaning parts but inevitably there were some hiccups along the way. Welcome help came from the then managing director of the Hill, Norman and Beard Organ Company who was willing to take on the ongoing maintenance.

Tony was determined to have the organ playable for the Church's dedication service planned for 15th October 1977. To achieve this he had to persuade his employers, the Post Office, to allow him to take four weeks unpaid special leave. With the help of others and long hours of working, the organ was playable for the dedication service. 'It was the first time most people had heard it for at least six years. There was much rejoicing in the service and afterwards at the celebration meal!' (Dunhill 2016, p.40). Jean Murphy has a recollection of that very special moment. Betty Osborne in her account of the consecration service says, 'what a joy it was to hear the organ'. She also describes how the three verses of the opening hymn 'O enter thou His gates with praise' were not nearly long enough to accompany the procession into the Church and the seating of all involved so, 'the organist had to improvise for a very long time before everyone had been accommodated' (Osborne 1978). This was something that Tony was well able to do. Rev. John Williams continued to play the organ himself during services. In recent years, although the piano is used most of all, there are visiting organists who treat us to the wonderful sound of the organ, and one who regularly visits to practise on the organ.

Pianos and More

By the early 1970s the Church hall was being used for most services because of all the problems in the Church. Tony Dunhill describes music in the hall services: 'When we first moved into the hall for services, we sang hymns to the accompaniment of a piano, and psalms and canticles to an ancient harmonium. The harmonium (fortunately) fell by the wayside, and we subsequently acquired a grand piano' (Dunhill 2016, p.28). In the new St Saviour's, Tony put on occasional musical evenings which Jean Murphy remembers attending. 'These always included some organ and piano music solos, but also singing and instrumental music created with other friends' (Dunhill 2016, p.14). The DCC minutes for 25th February 1982 record an agreement to purchase a new grand piano from Morley's for £3000 and it was Tony who organised the purchase on behalf of St Saviour's.

Ray Vincent recalls that in the 1980s the morning service had a group of young people who played a range of instruments including guitars, French horns, flutes, violins and piano. In recent times Andy Spraggs was pianist for some years. Following this the Church has employed young pianists who are part of a network of drama and music school students and graduates. But now we are fortunate the Reverend Henry's wife, Hillary, is a very able piano player and increasingly also his son, Nathaniel. In recent years we have also had occasional accompaniment on a variety of instruments from Ray and Pat's children and grandchildren, and children and young people from the Church who play the piano and ukulele. Miriam Gordon has played the clarinet at some services including the Carols by Candlelight service. Drum accompaniment was provided by Mike Kitts and since his death a member of St John's Stratford attends regularly to help out with drum accompaniment. Other percussion instruments often accompany the singing.

Choir

A common problem across the history of the Church has been difficulties in getting the numbers ideally required to form a full choir. In the parish magazine for September 1905 we read that a notice has been placed in the porch of what would have been the old St Saviour's Church appealing for new members:

> In view of the heavy work anticipated during the coming winter, the choirmaster will be glad to receive the names of ten gentlemen who will give their services in our choir, both bass and tenor, who are communicants. A knowledge of music is necessary.
>
> It is desired that only those gentlemen will volunteer who can see their way to maintain a regular attendance at the services on Sunday, and practice of one hour's duration on Fridays.

At the PCC meeting of 30th August 1957 a concern to increase the number of choristers is noted: 'Mrs Barnard says she has approached several young people without success'.

As already mentioned Tony Dunhill became choirmaster when he joined St Saviour's in the 1960s and Ray Vincent remembers that there was a 'thriving' choir at that time. Jean Murphy who started to regularly attend St Saviour's in the 1970s was in the choir. Albert and Anne Gordon remember that their daughter was in the choir. At this time the choir wore blue robes and, in the new St Saviour's, used the room opposite the vestry room to store robes, and this was where the choir changed into their robes. The choir gathered in an area to the left of the Altar.

Rev. John Williams asked Andy Spraggs to lead worship at St Saviour's in 2005 not long after Andy had received some intimation of this in his first visit to New Wine. He was surprised that John knew about his musical abilities because, although he attended St Saviour's as a child, from 1979 until 2004 school and then university had taken him to other areas. Andy became choir leader and pianist and also accompanied on guitar. Mike Kitts, who very sadly died suddenly in 2018, was an expert drummer and very committed in his attendance. Choir practice was on Friday evening and also from 10am on Sundays, half an hour before the service began, and Mike drove every week from Chelmsford for the practice and again for the Sunday service.

The choir was only a handful of people. Deborah Fisher started attending St Saviour's regularly as a result of joining the choir in 2012. She recalls the high standard set by Andy and Mike in the two practices each week and was pleased to learn so many songs new to her. Miriam Gordon was pleased that she was encouraged to join, and able to rejoin the choir during her university holidays. Miriam and her sister, Leah, continue to lead us in the singing of worship songs.

Andy always regarded it as 'a pleasure and privilege' to lead worship at St Saviour's and play and worship at other churches in the local community. 'The whole of the time I was at St Saviour's, since 2004 until the time I left, was a time of great spiritual growth and blessing for me.'

Singing Not Allowed!

Singing is a particularly important part of the service and worship at St Saviour's, and of course something that the whole congregation is involved in, many knowing the songs off by heart. There are occasions when we sing a capella. Sometimes new songs are learned together as part of the service. But for many months in 2020 the Church was unusually silent, closed in the enforced lockdowns brought about by the Covid-19 pandemic. Singing went on in individual homes as members participated in services streamed via Facebook and You Tube. When services resumed in August 2020, singing was considered unsafe even when masked. We listened to worship songs via YouTube and it was difficult to resist accompanying them. Following a mass vaccination programme, the gradual reduction of restrictions from spring 2021 onwards, culminating in removal of most restrictions on 19th July 2021, meant that singing could joyfully return. But even then different conditions such as numbers of people and amount of ventilation needed to be considered. The Church of England guidance issued on 1st September 2021 still advised precautions in such situations. And in 2022 some continue to wear masks as Covid infections, thankfully less serious, continue to spread. The guidance is being regularly updated (Church of England 2022).

Technical Support

Ability to hear clearly all those participating in the delivery of services is of course much valued by Church members. When congregations started to return to church in 2020 and 2021 following the easing of restrictions during the Covid-19 pandemic, but still having to be well spaced, microphones and good sound systems proved even more essential.

But in the archives and the annual report for 1959-60 we come across a story of some disappointment for the Church when it decided to celebrate its 75th anniversary in 1959 with a plan to install a speech reinforcing system and also a 'chimes without bells system' in the bell tower. An appeal would be launched to support this but the cost would have been considerable and the Diocesan Advisory Council considered it unnecessary to have the system, and would not agree to the installation of synthetic bells. The report comments, 'the occasion of our birthday did not go unmarked although with less ceremony than we had hoped'. The Bishop of Barking preached at a special service and as an alternative, and to tangibly mark the anniversary, an appeal was launched for refurbishments to the pulpit.

In recent years Andy Spraggs, pianist and choir leader, and his wife Marie, who was then Marie Duggan, organised the sound system for the Friday practice and the Sunday service and Leah Gordon took on managing the presentation system. When Andy and Marie moved to another church, the then drummer, Mike Kitts, took over setting up the audio/sound system each week. This was then taken on by Hillary Henry increasingly aided by younger members of the congregation, while Leah has continued to help with the presentation equipment stepping in when necessary. The sound system is now ably overseen by the curate's husband Attlee Brathwaite. The vicar's son, Nathaniel, has taken a lead in organising the streaming of services, with the assistance of Emmanuel Nyarko Dei and with operating the presentation system. Long-time member Geoff Eze has been a constant in providing technical know-how in the inevitable times when equipment breaks down or needs updating.

Parish Magazine

The parish magazine, as with so many churches, was an essential communication tool. It was a key source of information about the church and its activities, and provided a forum for sharing experiences and ideas as well as for creative output such as poetry. Often members who moved would continue to subscribe to the magazine as a way of staying connected with the Church. In 2018 St Saviour's made the decision, after some consideration, to cease publishing its parish magazine *The Way*. It was becoming clearer that in an age of competing forms and sources of information it no longer had the same role in keeping Church membership informed and engaged. And it was no longer viable to use it to reach out to the local community in the same way as in the past. Jean Murphy resigned in 2014 after editing the magazine, with the help of other Church members, for 30 years. The role of editor was then taken over by another Church member Kathleen Rowe, before the final decision was made.

The Rev. Henry then produced a newsletter every Sunday which combined information for the service with information about upcoming events. With the outbreak of the Covid-19 pandemic this has translated into a combined service and information sheet initially introduced as an infection reduction measure to avoid circulation of song books or Communion books. The format can also easily be circulated by email to accompany online streamed services.

But as we looked through parish records we realised that difficult decisions and uncertainties about the magazine were something that cropped up regularly in some of the decades we are focussing on, and before. It seemed a particularly difficult time from the mid-1950s to the mid-1960s. Production methods were of course more limited in earlier decades. Examples of concerns over the years are:

In the minutes of the PCC meeting for 5th July 1938 it is recorded that 500 copies of the magazine were printed, of which 320 were sold. The costs for printing and the 'Homewords' inset exceeded revenue from sales and advertisements. It was proposed to obtain estimates from various printers, and for varying numbers of pages and to get specimen copies of different insets.

In the minutes of 16th March 1954 we learn that 300 copies of the magazine are circulated. By March 1955 this drops very slightly and the deficit continues. Over the next few months there are repeated discussions and various suggestions put forward for improving the magazine, including setting up a dummy issue with alternative advertising schemes.

On the 5th September 1956 a special council meeting is held to consider the future of the parish magazine. After a 'lengthy discussion', suggestions made range from the issue of a duplicated news sheet, instead of a magazine, to enlargement of the magazine to include more news pages and local advertisements. The price of the magazine is increased by one (old) penny (1d) to four pennies (4d).

By December 1957 the circulation has dropped to 265 copies. By October 1958 there is a further rise in printing costs and the vicar proposes 'that the whole question of the magazine be gone into by the Standing Committee'. There is some good news at the meeting on 13th March 1961. This time sales exceeded expenses and the circulation is now 235. The profit is down to the use of duplication instead of printing. However by November the magazine income is decreasing and the cost of production rising.

When John Williams becomes vicar at the first meeting he chairs, 5th August 1965, he highlights the importance of the effectiveness of the magazine and undertakes to look at giving it a 'face-lift'. At the meeting of 25th October 1965 the vicar presents his plan for a new parish magazine, a slightly larger page size but same number of pages, 400 copies to be printed instead of duplicated. The vicar offers to be responsible for any deficit for a trial period of one year. A deficit is registered in January 1966, over the past year expense has been £48, 7 shillings and 9 pence and income £41, 19 shillings and 5 pence.

We know the magazine continues. Methods of production were changing including the ability to type up, photocopy and put together the magazine at base. Though equally the opportunities for getting advertising support was reducing as other avenues for advertising increased.

And So It Continues...

This little history of St Saviour's will no doubt serve to prompt other memories of experiences and events, and perhaps corrections to the information presented here. The intention certainly is to continue to gather material to add to the Church's archive and to our understanding and appreciation of the history of St Saviour's and its place in the local community across many years and into the future.

Meanwhile we return to voices from the past. Although the words might seem old-fashioned, the beliefs and hopes expressed for the Church, its membership and community in this prayer and letter from past events, are as meaningful and as heartfelt today.

Part of the prayers said at the service for the opening of the church hall, 21st October 1904:

Almighty and most merciful God, we yield Thee hearty thanks that it hath pleased Thee to enable us thus far to complete the work we have undertaken, and to preserve us alive this day to give thanks to Thy Name. We bless Thee, the Lord both of the dead and the living, for those Thy servants into whose hearts Thou hast put it to work for and contribute towards the erection of the Hall. We ask Thy blessing on all who have and are in any way engaged in it. And now, O Lord, we beseech Thee to accept our offering and the work of our hands, and to sanctify this building to its sacred purpose: and because without Thy heavenly teaching all earthly teaching is vain, bless the labours of the teachers who shall teach here to the spiritual instruction and edification of those who shall come to learn; so that all may be taught of Thee, and remembering that One is their Master, even Christ, may through

Him be made wise unto salvation, who liveth and reigneth with Thee and the Holy Ghost, one God, world without end . *Amen*

Part of a letter from the vicar (Rev. B C Aldis) describing the repair and re-opening of the Church in 1949 following bomb damage:

For 65 years your parish church has stood here and has been a constant witness to the saving power of Jesus Christ. In these years hundreds of men, women and children have in this church found Jesus Christ as Saviour and friend, and have started in His strength to live a new life.

We still have the same message of Pardon, Peace and Power, which is of such vital importance to you and to all the world. Come and join with us, and make our dream come true of this Church as a place where many shall find the Saviour, shall come in to worship Him, and shall go out to serve Him.

(St Saviour's Church Forest Gate Year Book 1949-50)

Sources and References

Most of the information within this booklet comes from the parish records and other Church archives, and the memories of Church members. These sources are referred to throughout the text but not treated as citations.

The key parish records used are: *Annual Parochial Meetings + Vestry meetings 1952-2016 (referred to as AGM's in the text); Parochial Church Council (PCC) meetings March 1936-May 1953; PCC meetings July 1953-Dec 1968; PCC meetings Feb 1969- March 1989; PCC meetings 1989-2003; District Church Council meetings 1975-1987; District Church Council meetings 1982-2000*

Church /Parish Magazines: the only ones that still exist are bound copies of the *Church Monthly Magazine from 1904 to 1923*; two *Parish Magazines* from the 1960s; and a handful of very recent copies of *'The Way: Magazine of St Saviour's Forest Gate with St James Stratford'*.

Other archives:
British Newspaper Archive, The British Library https://www. bl.uk/collection-guides/british-newspaper-archive ;
Essex Record Office https://www.essexrecordoffice.co.uk/
London Metropolitan Archives https://search.lma.gov.uk/
Newham Archives and Local Studies Library https://www. newham.gov.uk/libraries-arts-culture/local-history-archives

References

BHO: British History Online (1973) 'West Ham: Education', in *A History of the County of Essex: Volume 6*, ed. W R Powell

(London, 1973), pp. 144-157. *British History Online* http://
www.british-history.ac.uk/vch/essex/vol6/pp144-157 [Accessed
8 May 2022].

Chelmsford Chronicle (1882) St. Saviour's Church, Forest Gate.
Laying the Foundation Stone in *Chelmsford Chronicle* 3rd Nov
p.5 accessed via the British Newspaper Archive, The British
Library Board. Available at www.britishnewspaperarchive.co.uk
[Accessed 25 August 2022]

Cherry, Bridget, O'Brien, Charles & Pevsner, Nikolaus (2005) *The
Buildings of England: London 5: East.* New Haven, CT; London:
Yale University Press, p.244.

Church of England (2022) *Coronavirus (Covid-19) guidance.*
Available at https://www.churchofengland.org/resources/
coronavirus-covid-19-guidance#na. [Accessed 27 July 2022].

Dunhill, Anthony (2016) *Making Music: the story of my interest
in music and instrument making.* 3rd ed. Anthony Dunhill.

E7 Now and Then (2017) *Samuel Gurney (1786 - 1856) - Forest
Gate's most influential resident.* Available at http://www.
e7-nowandthen.org/2017/12/samuel-gurney-1786-1856-forest-
gates.html [Accessed 16 April 2020].

E7 Now and Then (2018a) *Archibald Cameron Corbett - the man
and his houses -synopsis of film.* Available at http://www.
e7-nowandthen.org/2018/06/archibald-cameron-corbett-man-
and-his.html [Accessed 16 April 2020].

E7 Now and Then (2018b) *Emmanuel church (2) - rapid rise and
fall of the Church of England in Forest Gate.* Available at http://
www.e7-nowandthen.org/2018/09/emmanuel-church-2-rapid-
rise-and-fall.html [Accessed 28 April 2020].

E7 Now and Then (2018c) *Racism in Forest Gate in the 1970s
and 1980s Part 1.* Available at http://www.e7-nowandthen.

org/2018/06/racism-in-forest-gate-in-1970s-and.html [Accessed 15 February 2020]).

Essex Record Office. *Record Reference: D/P 631Forest Gate, St Saviour.* Available at https://www.essexarchivesonline.co.uk/Result_Details.aspx?DocID=741106 [Accessed 24 July 2022].

Essex Record Office. *Record Reference: D/P 631/6/5 Form of Service for the Opening of St Saviour's Hall. Friday Afternoon October 21, 1904.*

Faith in Schools (2022) *Knife Crime Project.* Available at https://www.faithinschools.co.uk/knife-crime-project [Accessed 11 July 2022].

Falkner, Sophia (2021) *Knife Crime in the Capital: How gangs are drawing another generation into a life of crime.* London: Policy Exchange. Available at https://policyexchange.org.uk/publication/knife-crime-in-the-capital/ [Accessed 18 May 2022].

Francis, Leslie J and Roberts, Carol (2009) *Growth or decline in the Church of England during the Decade of Evangelism: did the churchmanship of the bishop matter?* University of Warwick institutional repository. Available at http://wrap.warwick.ac.uk/2877/1/WRAP_Francis_0673558-ie-170210-decade_of_evangelism_mla.pdf [Accessed 27 July 2022]
Final article available in the Journal of Contemporary Religion Vol.24 pp.67-81.

Gorman, Mark (2021) *Saving the People's Forest: Open spaces, enclosure and popular protest in mid-Victorian London.* Hatfield: University of Hertfordshire Press (Explorations in Local and Regional History Vol.9).

Honeybone, Ben (2018)*Archibald Cameron Corbett: The Man and the Houses* [Film]. *The Corbett Society.* Available at https://thecorbettsociety.org.uk/film/ [Accessed 26 June 2020].

Johnson, Carol (2003) Village Life. *Forest Gate Times* September? P.6

Kvist, Elsa (2012) Vicar retires after 46 years at same church in Forest Gate. *Newham Recorder* 14 October. Available at https://www.newhamrecorder.co.uk/news/vicar-retires-after-46-years-at-same-church-in-forest-gate-1-1655224 [Accessed 30 June 2020].

London Borough of Newham (2009) *Forest Gate Town Centre Conservation Area: Character Appraisal and Management Proposals March 2009*. Available at https://www.newham.gov.uk/downloads/file/920/forest-gate-conservation-area-appraisal-proposals [Accessed 16 March 2022].

London City Mission n.d. *The Story of London City Mission* [Film]. Available at https://www.lcm.org.uk/our-mission/history [Accessed 27 July 2020].

Loudon, Lois (2012) *Distinctive and Inclusive: The National Society and Church of England Schools, 1811-2011*. London: The National Society.

Osborne, Betty (1978) A New Beauty: Consecration of the Parish Church of St Saviour, Forest Gate.No source given but probably *St Saviour's Church Parish Magazine* (Article in Newham Archive and Local Studies Library, marked 1978 but may be 1977).

Pooley, C.G. and Turnbull, J. (1997) Changing home and workplace in Victorian London: the life of Henry Jaques, Shirtmaker in *Urban History* 24(2) pp.148-178 . Lancaster EPrints, Lancaster University. Available at https://eprints.lancs.ac.uk/id/eprint/31418/1/download1.pdf [Accessed 30 March 2020].

Stratford Express (1888a) St Saviour's Church Debt. *Stratford Express* 13th October p.3 accessed via the British Newspaper Archive, The British Library Board. Available at www.britishnewspaperarchive.co.uk [Accessed 25 August 2022].

Stratford Express (1888b) St Saviour's Church of England Temoperance Society. *Stratford Express* 13th October p.3 accessed via the British Newspaper Archive, The British Library Board. Available at www.britishnewspaperarchive.co.uk [Accessed 25 August 2022].

Wanstead Flats Working Group (2017) *Turf Wars: the Struggle to Cultivate Wanstead Flats.* London: Leyton and Leytonstone Historical Society.

Wanstead Flats Working Group (2019) *Religion and Revolt on Wanstead Flats.* London: Leyton and Leytonstone Historical Society.

Wikipedia (2022) *Forest Gate railway station.* Available at https://en.wikipedia.org/wiki/Forest_Gate_railway_station [Accessed 6 June 2020]).

Wikipedia (2022) *St James Church, Forest Gate.* Available at https://en.wikipedia.org/wiki/St_James%27_Church,_Forest_Gate [Accessed 3 July 2020].

Wilson, Andrew (1995) *That Big Church on the Corner: A History of Emmanuel Church Forest Gate.* London: P.C.C. of Emmanuel Church.

Woods, Frederick William (1934) *St. Saviour's Parish Church 1884-1934. A short account of its history. Jubilee Year.* London: Wards, Woodgrange Press Ltd.

Appendix: Key Dates in the History of St Saviour's Church

Date	Event
1880	St Saviour's is established as a daughter church of Emmanuel Church, Romford Road. Mission services are held by Rev. Henderson Burnside in the Forest Gate National School at the corner of Forest Street and Woodgrange Road on land donated by Samuel Gurney
1880	St Saviour's and the school move into an iron building in Macdonald Road (next to where the Church is now)
1882 November 1st	The Foundation Stone is laid for a more substantial building for St Saviour's designed by the architect Edwin Clare FRIBA and sited at the corner of Macdonald and Station Roads
1884 April 1st	St Saviour's is consecrated by the Bishop of St Albans, Bishop Claughton
1884 August 11th	Order-in-Council establishes the formation of a separate parish for St Saviour's previously part of Emmanuel's parish
1892	The iron building in Macdonald Road is demolished
1904 June 17th October 21st	St Saviour's church hall is built and opened The foundation stone is laid by Alfred F Buxton The hall, designed by F Danby Smith ARIBA, is opened by the Lord Bishop of St Albans
1910	The vicarage is built in Sidney Road

Date	Event
1934	Booklet published to commemorate the Jubilee of the consecration of St Saviour's. The booklet is organised according to the different vicars in post over that period
1944 October	Church closed due to bomb damage and its on-going effects. Services take place in the hall, 'which, although it did not escape damage was readily convertible into a church, and was duly licensed by the Bishop'
1949 July 2nd	'Re-opening Service' following repairs to the damage caused by bomb and its consequences
1959	75th anniversary of consecration of St Saviour's. Plan to install a new sound system and a 'chimes without bells' system is turned down by the Diocese. Appeal launched instead for refurbishment of pulpit
1975	St Saviour's and St Matthew's, Dyson Road, are united in a combined parish with St Saviour's as the parish church
1975 July	Demolition of original St Saviour's
1977 October 15th	Consecration of the 'new' St Saviour's in the refurbished and re-modelled church hall
1980	Centenary of founding of St Saviour's celebrated with some special events including a renewal of marriage vows service and a Parish Week. Other events planned included a Shrove Tuesday pancake party, a concert and a barbecue and disco!
2013 October	The parishes of St Saviour and St Matthew are separated

ST SAVIOUR'S CHURCH, FOREST GATE: CELEBRATING 140 YEARS

Date	Event
2014 October 1st	St Saviour's re-named St Saviour's with St James. Part of the parish of St John and Christ Church, Stratford, with St James, including the former church of St James' (since demolished) transferred to St Saviour's
2017 September 16th	Church marks 40th anniversary of its consecration as the 'new' St Saviour's with a dinner and barn dance